LATER INDO-SCYTHIANS

LATER INDO-SCYTHIANS

MAJOR-GENERAL SIR A. CUNNINGHAM,
R.E., K.C.I.E., C.S.I., &c.

GYAN

Published by

Gyan Publishing House
5, Ansari Road
Daryaganj, New Delhi-110002
Phone: 011-47034999, 9811692060
E-mail: books@gyanbooks.com

Distribution Network
gyanbooks.com
India, USA, Canada, UK, Australia, France

ISBN : 978-81-212-2570-0 (HB)
First Published, 1893

2nd Impression 2021

Printed at: Gyan Press, Delhi.

Later Indo-Scythians
Author: Major-General Sir A. Cunningham

LATER INDO-SCYTHIANS.

BY

MAJOR-GENERAL SIR A. CUNNINGHAM, R.E.,

K.C.I.E., C.S.I.

REPRINTED FROM THE NUMISMATIC CHRONICLE,

VOL. XIII., THIRD SERIES, PAGES 93—128.

LONDON:

1893.

PREFACE.

(By E. J. RAPSON, M.A.)

THE papers collected together in this volume appeared periodically in the *Numismatic Chronicle* during the years 1893 and 1894. The last of the series, which deals with the history and numismatics of the White Huns, as published after the author's death; but, as it is ractically a reprint of an article included in the *Transactions of the Oriental Congress of* 1892, it, too, may be said to have had the benefit of his final revision.

General Sir Alexander Cunningham has elsewhere treated of the earlier foreign settlers—Greeks, Ṣakas, and Kushâns—the traces of whose dominion in India have afforded so much help in the recovery of its lost history. He here extends this investigation to the later and less-known Indo-Scythian dynasties, whose dates range from about the end of the second century to the middle of the seventh century A.D. Of the coinages of these later Indo-Scythian rulers no scientific classification has previously been attempted. The arrangement here proposed marks a distinct advance in Indian chronology, for which students of Indian history and archæology will be grateful.

No careful reader of the following pages can fail to recognise in this, the author's last work, the qualities which characterise everything that he wrote—his unequalled knowledge of Indian numismatics, his intimate acquaintance with the many sources from which has been gleaned whatever is now known of the history of Ancient and Mediæval India, and his great natural acumen.

I have added an Index, which I hope will facilitate reference to the work.

British Museum,
7th Feb., 1895.

[The thanks of the late Genl. Sir Alexander Cunningham' sons are due to Mr. E. J. Rapson for his care in preparin the Table of Contents, Preface, and Index of this work, and thereby rendering it more useful to readers.]

LATER INDO-SCYTHIANS.

(See Plates VIII.—X.)

INTRODUCTION.

THE earliest immigrations which have left any permanent traces in India were made from the north-east by the Dravidians, who occupied Southern India; and from the north-west by the Brahüis, who occupied the country on the Lower Indus. They were followed by the Aryas, who overran all Northern India, and introduced the Brahmanical religion, which still exists, though in a much altered form.

The Persian invasions of Cyrus and Darius, and the Greek invasion of Alexander affected only the valley of the Indus and its tributaries. Each occupation lasted for only a few centuries. But the successive Scythian invasions of the *Sakas*, the *Kushâns*, and the *White Huns*, were followed by permanent settlements of large bodies of their countrymen, which lasted for many centuries, and which can still be traced in the names of the countries which they occupied. Thus the name of the *Sakas* was imposed on Drangiana as *Sakastene*, now Sistan, and their language was still spoken in the tenth century as the *Sakri*. The name of the *Kushâns* is still preserved in the *Koresh* tribes of Kâfiristan under their ruler, "Shah *Kitor*," and their language is still spoken as the *Kâfiri*. The name of the *Jâbuli* tribe of White Huns is still preserved in Zâbulistan, and their language still existed in the tenth century as the *Zâüli*.

The history of these three races can be traced from the date of their first appearance down to the present day. But there are other foreign races in the north-west of India, the date of whose occupation is quite unknown. The best known and the most numerous of these foreign races are the *Gakars*, the *Jâts*, the *Gujars*, and the *Ahîrs*.

The *Gakars* declare that they came from *Kaiân*, in *Khorasân*, in the time of Afrasiâb. They claim descent from *Kîd* or *Kaid*, and assert that they held Kashmir for sixteen generations. Their first appearance under their present name was in the reign of Mahmud of Ghazni, whom they opposed with thirty thousand men, as allies of Anang-pâl. In A.D. 1205 they killed Muhammad Ghori in his tent on the banks of the Indus; and half a century later they offered a most stubborn resistance to the Emperor Balban. They were at last subdued, and their ruler, *Kokâr Sankâ*, became a Musulmân. In the beginning of the sixteenth century they opposed Bâber, but were reduced to submission. The whole of the hilly country between the Indus and Jhelam, known better by the name of the Jûd Mountains, or Mount Jûd, was then held by "two races descended from the same father, who from old times had been rulers of the hills between Nilâb and Bhira." "On one half of the hill" (says Bâber) "lived the Jûd, and on the other half the Janjûha." The people here called the *Jûd* must be apparently the *Gakars*, as Bâber adds that they and the Janjûhas were "old enemies." At that time the chief of the Gakars bore the title of *Malik Hast*, which was an old designation, as I find it used by the bard Chand in his Prithi-Râj Râsa, under the slightly altered form of the "*Gakar Malik Hath*." No derivation is given for the name; but I think it probable that the Gakars may be the *Gargaridæ* of Alexander's historians.[1] *Gharghara*, the "rumbler or gurgler," is the Sanskrit name of the *Gagar* or *Kagar* River, near Ambâla, and of the *Ghâgra* River of Oudh. This title of *Hast* or *Hath* is probably connected with the *Hyst* of *Hyst*aspes, the *Vist* of *Vist*aspa, and with the *Bist* of *Bist*ax, and the *Vit* of *Vit*axæ, which was a royal title, as Hesychius says, ὁ Βασιλεὺς παρὰ Πέρσαις. It was equivalent to the Indian *Aswapati*, "lord of horses," a common title for kings. Another form is ΠΙΤΥΑΞΗΣ. The title of *Malik Hast*, or *Hath*, gives a strong support to the claim of the Gakars as immigrants from Khorasân. The same name is applied to the Gandgarh, or *Ghargar* Mountains, to the north-west of Râwal Pindi, from which *rumbling* sounds are believed to issue from imprisoned demons. From this mountain the *Gakars* may have received their names, just as they got the name of *Jûd* from the Muhammadans. But if there is any truth in their claim to be immigrants from Khorasân, *Gakar* could not have been their original name. They were probably *Abars* from *Abar-shahr* (or Nishapur), the old capital of Khorasân, and it is not impossible that they may have been a colony transported by Darius into the Panjâb to hold his new Indian conquest. The earliest settlement is said by some to have been at *Abriyân* or *Abariân*.

The *Jâts* in old times are said to have divided Sindh with the Meds. They are now very numerous in the Panjâb, and in the districts to the east of the Satlej; and they form the bulk of the Sikh nation. Lassen has iden-

---

[1] Dionys., *Perieg. V.* 1144, mentions the *Gargaridæ* after the Peukanei and Toxili.

tified them with the *Jârttikas* of the Mahâbhârata, before the Christian era. Perhaps they may be the *Iatii* of Pliny. Our first notices of the *Jâts* are due to the plundering raids made by the early Muhammadans of Sistan and Mekran into Sindh in the latter half of the seventh century A.D. At that time the kingdom of Sindh embraced the whole valley of the Indus and its tributaries from the foot of the Kashmir Mountains to the sea, and from the east direct to the borders of Mekran and Khorasân. Sindh here divided into four provinces—I. Multan on the north; II. Brâhmanâbâd on the south; III. Ashkalanda on the east; and IV. Sivistan on the west. The most exposed province was *Kikân*, which formed the southern part of Sivistan. Its capital was, Kandâbil or Gandhâva, with Kosdar on the south and Kilât on the west. This district was famous for a fine breed of large horses, which are specially noted by the Chinese pilgrim, Hwen Thsang, as well as by the Muhammadan historians. The people are called *Jâts* and *Meds*, and as they are described as *Samânis*, or Buddhists, I infer that to their religious belief was due the name of *Buddha* for the district.

The *Jâts* and *Meds* are described in the *Mujmal at-Tawârikh* as being the most ancient inhabitants of the country. In the notices of the early Muhammadan writers the former would appear to have been more numerous in the north and west, while the latter, who stretched down to the sea, held the east and south. It seems probable, therefore, that the *Meds* may have given their name to *Medapâta*, or Mevâr, and that their present representatives may be the *Mers* of *Merwân* in the Aravali range of mountains. The *Jàts*, who are all Muhammadans, are still very numerous in the Panjâb, and along the Indus, while the Indian branch, or *Jâts*, who are all Hindus, are very numerous between the Satlej and the Jumna. The Sikh Rajas of Patiâla, Jhind, and Nabha are Jâts, and so are the Raja of Bharatpur and the Râna of Dholpur on the Chambal.

The name of Kikân or Kaikân, or Kaikânân I believe to be as old as the time of Darius, in whose inscription there is mention of a fort in Arachosia called *Kâpishkânish*, where the rebel Veisdatu fought a battle with the Satrap Vibanus. As the Greek *Kambistholi* and the Sanskrit *Kapisthala* have been shortened to *Kaithal*, so *Kaikân* may be accepted as a regular abbreviation of the Persian *Kâpishkânish* and the Scythian *Kâppissâkânis*. As it was a fort I would identify it with *Kilât*, the capital of Baluchistân. The rebel Satrap also fought a second battle in Arachosia at *Gadutawa*, or *Kautuvata*, which I would identify with *Gandâva* of the present day, and with *Kandâbil* of the early Muhammadan writers.

The *Gujars* are scattered all over the Panjâb and the Gangetic Provinces. Their chief settlement was in the province which was named after them *Gurjarâshtra*. In the Panjâb their name still survives in the town of *Gujarât*.

The *Ahîrs* are also scattered over Northern India. Their full name was *Abhîra*, which they still held in the time of Alexander, who found them on the Lower Indus. The only place that now bears their name is the district of *Ahîrwara*, in the Gwalior territory. General Baptiste changed the name to *Isagarh*, but the people adhere to the old name.

The date of the great Aryan migration, which gave the dominant races to Persia and India, is uncertain. Roughly, it may be placed some twenty centuries before the Christian era. In Persia the Aryas were firmly settled in all the provinces. We find them in Media, Hyrkania, and Khorasmia; in Bactria and Sogdiana; and in Aria, Drangiana, and Arakhosia. In India we find them in the people of Gândhâra and Sattagydia, in the Assakani of the Kabul valley, and in the descendants of *Jajâti* (or Gegasios, Γηγάσιος), the Yâdavas, the Pauravas, and the Anavas of the Panjâb.

From *Yadu* sprang the *Aswakas* or *Assakani*, who have been identified by Professor Lassen with the Aoghâns or Afghâns. From *Puru* came the *Pândavas* (the *Pandovi* of Ptolemy), and the *Paurava king Porus*, whose posterity are now represented by the *Pândava* Rajputs of the Panjâb hills. From *Anu* sprang the *Anava* tribes of the *Sauviras*, the *Kaikeyas* and the *Madras*, with the *Yaudheyas* and their kinsmen the *Janjûhas*. The *Sauviras* of Sindhu Suvira most probably gave their name to Σωφιρά, or *Ophir*. The *Madras* gave their name to *Madr-des*, which is still used for the Doâb between the Chenâb and Râvi, which Akbar afterwards called the *Richna Doâb*. The *Yaudheyas* or *Jodhiyas* are now the *Johiyas* of the Salt Range and the Lower Panjâb, where the tract above Multân is still called the *Johiya-bâr*. The *Janjûhas* still exist under the same name, or in its shortened form of *Janûha*, in the district of *Potawâr*, between the Indus and the Jhelam.

The Aryan settlements in North India were still incomplete in the time of the Vedas and the Mahâbhârata, or from about B.C. 1500 to 1200, when their territories were bounded by the *Karmanâsa* River (or *Karmnâsa*) in the east, and by the *Varnanâsa* River (or *Banâs*) on the south. The passage of both these streams was forbidden to the Aryas, as the crossing of the first would be the "destroyer" (*nâsa*) of *Karma*, or good works; and the crossing of the second would be the destroyer of *varna*, or "caste." The prohibition about the *Karmnâsa* survived in full force down to the present century, when villagers were still employed to carry passengers over the stream, to save them from getting wetted. Their employment has ceased since the bridge was built.

Before the irruptions of the Indo-Scythians the valleys of the Oxus, the Helmand, and the Indus had been overrun by Cyrus, by Darius, and by Alexander; and to their expeditions is due almost all our early knowledge of those countries. Briefly they may be described as comprising Bactriana, Ariana, and North-west India.

The earliest notices that we possess are the campaigns of Cyrus, and the inscriptions of Darius. Kapisa, the capital of Kapissene, in Ariana, is said to have been destroyed by Cyrus, while the Assakeni, to the west of the Indus, are said to have submitted to him and paid tribute.[2] But in his campaign against the Sacæ, or Sakas, on the Jaxartes, he was defeated, and either killed or captured. Herodotus calls these Scythians Massagetæ, but he admits that some regard them as *Sacæ*, or Sakas.[3] Ktesias calls them *Sacæ*, and gives the names of their king and queen as Amorges and Sparethra. From the name of the king I infer that his people were the Amurgii Scythæ of Herodotus, and the *Sakâ Humawarkâ* of the inscriptions of Darius. The queen is named Tomyris by Herodotus, and her son *Spargapeises*. The two names of *Sparethra* and *Spargapeises* I would compare with *Spalahora*, *Spalirisha*, *Spalgadama*, and *Sapaleizes* of our well-

[2] Plin. *Nat. Hist.* vi. 25, and Arrian, *Indica*, I.

[3] Herodotus, I. 205, calls the queen *Tomyris*. Ktesias alone calls her Sparethra.

known Saka coins; and I conclude that the Saka-Scythians of the Jaxartes, with whom Cyrus came into contact, were the ancestors of the *Sakas* who long afterwards established themselves in Sakastene or Sejistan, and not the *Massagetæ*.

With the inscriptions of Darius, B.C. 520—490, we reach the firmer ground of real history. He was an administrator as well as a conqueror, and every country that he subdued was added permanently to the Persian empire. In the Naksh-i-Rustem inscription he names the eastern provinces in the following order:—

> Parthia, Aria; Bactriana, Sogdiana, Khorasmia; Zarangia, Arakhosia, Sattagydia; Gandaria, India.

The revenue of each province was fixed, and governors were appointed, and about one century and a quarter later the whole empire passed into the possession of Alexander.

Before invading India Alexander the Great conquered Bactria and Sogdiana, where he came in contact with the Massagetæ and Dahæ. The Assakani then held the greater part of the Kabul Valley, with Massaga as their capital.[4] They possessed a large army of 20,000 horse, 30,000 foot, and 30 elephants. Their king Assakanus was killed in battle, and their queen Kleophis then surrendered the capital. Two brothers, named Kophæus and Aśsagetes, came in. As Assagân is only a plural form, meaning the nation or people called *Aswakas*, or *Assakas*, or the "Horsemen," it was suggested by Lassen that the *Assagani* were the actual ancestors of the present Afghans. In support of this suggestion I can refer to the fact that the people generally do not call themselves *Afghâns*, but

---

[4] *Arrian. Anab.* iv. 25, 26, and *Indica*, i.

Aoghâns, and that the Albanians are called *Aoghâns* by the Armenians.

As the Sanskrit *aswa* becomes *equus* in Latin, as *swasri* becomes *khwar*, or *khor*, in Pushtu, and as *Saraswati* becomes *Arakhoti* and *Harakhaiti*, so *Aswagân* became *Akhwagân*. In fact the old form of Afghân was Aoghân, and both Timur and his secretary write Aoghâni, and even Aghâni. The change from *l* to *gh* by the Armenians is found also in *Vagharsh*, for the Persian *Balash*.

I find that the name of *Albania* is given by Pliny to the country of the Indian Sophytes.[5] As the salt mines were in his territory, the name must have been applied to the country between the Jhelam and the Indus; and as the salt mines are found also at Kâlâbâgh, the name of *Albania* may have included territory to the west of the Indus.

According to Ammianus there were Alani, or Albani, to the east of the Caspian. When war broke out between Persia and Rome in the time of Sapor II., the Persian king was absent in his north-east frontier in hostilities with the Chionitæ and *Albani*. Both nations had powerful kings; and in the subsequent siege of Amida in A.D. 358, Sapor was very greatly assisted by their troops.[6]

It is in favour of the original name of Aswabeus that several districts in Afghanistan were famous for their breed of horses. Thus—

(1.) *Bannu*, the *Falana* of Hwen Thsang, gave its name to the "*Vanâyu-ja* horses," which were much esteemed.

(2.) On the eastern side of the Indus lies the district of *Dhăni*, where Runjit Singh had a breeding stud. Pânini

---

[5] *Plinii Nat. Hist.* viii. 61, and *Strabon.* xv. 1—30.

[6] *Ammian. Marcel.* xviii. 6, 21, and xix. 2, 3.

calls the country *Varnu,* with a river of the same name, which is the Bannu River of the present day.

(3.) When in Falana, the Chinese pilgrim Hwen Thsang notes that on the west, in *Ki-kiang-na,* the people had an immense number of sheep and horses, and that the horses were of large size and excellent. A few years later the early Muhammadan invaders were continually making raids into Kikân, or Kaikân, for the purpose of obtaining some of these famous steeds. Thus, in A.D. 664, Muhallab, when in Kikân, saw eighteen Turki horsemen on crop-tailed horses. The men fought with great gallantry, which Muhallab attributed to their horses, and accordingly *he docked the tails of all his own horses!* A few years later Abdullah presented a Kikân horse to the Khalif. Perhaps the name may have some connection with *kîkatâ,* a "horse." It is not improbable that it may be the mediæval form of *Kapishkanish,* a fort in Arakhosia, held by a rebel against Darius. In the same way that the Sanskrit *Kapisthala* has been shortened to *Kaithal,* so *Kapishkanish* may have become *Kaikân,* or *Kaikâna.*

(4.) Ferrier notices (*Afghans,* p. 297) the "splendid animals" of *Herat* and *Hazâra,* which are taken to India for sale to the cavalry and artillery.

At the present day all the people of Afghanistan, from the Indus on the east to the Heri-Rûd River on the west, speak Pushtu, or Pakhtu. But the clan which bears the name of Pushtun, or Pakhtun, claims to be distinct as the original speakers of the language. It is even affirmed that all the other clans who speak Pushtu are immigrants who have adopted the language. The name of *Paktüike,* or *Pakhtunka,* we know to be as old as the time of Darius; but the name of *Assakani* is equally old; and as the districts of the Paktyans and of the Assakani were in

Gândhâra, the language of both peoples was most probably the same.

But there is mention by Ktesias of another clan who must also have belonged to Gândhâra. These are the *καλύστριοι*, whose name is said to mean "dog-headed," or *κυνοκέφαλοι*. I accept the name of *Kalustrii* for reasons which I will give presently; and I look upon the asserted translation of "dog's head" as a mere nickname—perhaps by a slight alteration of a well-known Indian descriptive term. Thus *aswamukha*, or "horse-headed," might with some reason have been applied to the Eastern Ethiopians, who wore the scalps of horses for their head-dress, with the ears erect. By omitting the initial letter, the term would become *swâ-mukha*, or "dog-face." But whatever may have been the origin of the nickname of "dog's-heads," it is quite certain that *kalustrii* could not have that meaning. But Pliny mentions a people on the Lower Indus called *Salabastræ*, or *Arabastræ*, whose name might be the Indian *Kâla-vastra*, or "*Black-vests*," synonymous with the Persian *Siya-pash*, which is still applied to those people in Afghanistan who wear "black sheep-skin" dresses. As Ktesias specially notes that the name was given to them by the Indians, the derivation from *Kâla-vastrà*, or "Black-vests," seems a very natural one. Other details which Ktesias gives seem to fix the country of the Kalustrii beyond all possibility of doubt. "They inhabit," he says, "the mountains and extend as far as the river Indus." These mountains were "steep and pathless." The river *Hyparkhos* (Pliny says *Hypobares*[7]) flowed through their country. As this name is said to mean *φέρων πάντα τὰ ἀγαθὰ*, its more correct form would be

[7] *Plinii Nat. Hist.* xxxvii. 2.

Eubares, in Sanskrit, *Subhara*. On its banks grew a tree, called *siptakhora*, which bore a very sweet fruit, with a stone as large as a filbert nut. This fruit was dried and packed in plaited baskets, like raisins. This description points to the *shaft-âru*, or peach, and the *zard-âru*, or apricot, both of which grow in Afghanistan, where they are split open, dried, and packed in small baskets, or wooden punnets, for exportation.[8]

Two other products of the country of the Kalustrii seem equally well to fix its position to the west of the Indus. It produced "a purple flower, used for making a purple dye, not inferior to the Greek sort, but of a far more florid hue." This was the *manjîth*, or "madder." The other product was an insect which, when crushed to powder, yielded a purple dye, superior to that used by the Persians. This insect was the *coccus lacca*, or "lac insect." The "tears of gum, like amber," were, of course, derived from the cases of the *coccus lacca*, which are commonly known as "shell lac."

Thus all these products of the Kalustrii, as described by Ktesias, still form some of the staples of Afghanistan. The *dried fruits* packed like raisins, the *madder*, the *lac dye*, and the *shell lac* form part of the present traffic of the country, as I can personally vouch for.

A strong reason for my adoption of the name of *Kalustrii* without any alteration is the curious fact that it corresponds with that of the alphabet which was in use

---

[8] *Fragments of Ktesias*, translated by McCrindle, pp. 22—24. The animal which Ktesias calls *martikhora*, or "man-eater," is simply the well-known "wild goat," or *mârkhor*, the "snake-eater," which abounds in the Sulimâni Mountains of Afghanistan. As the Kalustrii by some slight alteration of name were believed to have heads like dogs, so the *mârkhor* had a head like a "man" (*mard* in Persian).

all over Gândhâra in Afghanistan for several centuries both before and after the Christian era. In the account of Buddha's education it is stated that the young prince Sakya Sinha was taught sixty-four different alphabets, of which three are distinguished by the direction of their writing.

I. *Brahma*—written from left to right.

II. *Kharosti*—written from right to left.

III. *Chinese*—written perpendicularly.

In the Chinese version of the Lalita Vistara the Kharosti (*Kai-lu-she-ti*) is said to mean "donkey's lips." But as the full name is *Kharoshtri*, as written by Dr. G. Bühler, it agrees letter for letter with the *Kalustrii* of Ktesias. The *Kharoshtri* script, which was written from right to left, would therefore be the alphabet of the *Kalustrii* of Gândhâra, to the west of the Indus. We thus learn that the name of the Gândharian script, which is found in the Western inscriptions of Asoka on both sides of the Indus, was called *Kharoshtri*. In my book on the *Coins of Ancient India* I have called it the *Gândharian* alphabet, a name which accurately describes the extent of country in which it was used—its earliest use, so far as is known at present, is in the inscriptions of Asoka, and on the Indian coins of Demetrius, the son of Euthydemus, which date from the third century B.C. But as it had already added the Indian vowel system with the aspirated consonants to its scanty Aramean original, it is certain that it must have been in use for a long time previous to Asoka. Dr. Isaac Taylor thinks that the original Aramean alphabet must have been introduced into Afghanistan and the Panjâb some time after the accession of Darius in B.C. 520. With this conclusion I cordially concur; and I would fix "the expansion of the alphabet with its simple vowel system and aspirates between 500 and 400 B.C., after its contact with the more fully developed system of the Indian alphabet."

The name of Kalustrii still remains to be explained. The "dogs' heads" of Ktesias and the "asses' lips" of the Chinese may be dismissed at once. At the present day there are two of the travelling merchant tribes of Afghans, the *Ushturis* and the *Kharotis*, who may perhaps still preserve the name. The former tribe live in "black tents," and might therefore be called *Kâloshtari* (*Kâla-vastra*), and the latter tribe, the *Kharoti*, give the general curtailed form of the name. Both tribes are engaged in the carrying trade, and both are included under the general names of *Povinda* and *Lohâni*, from the nature of their occupation. "They usually assemble in autumn in the plains of Zurmat, Gardez, and Kattawâz, to the east of Ghazni, and make their way through the passes to the Derajât, where they leave their families and flocks. The men go with their goods to India. These consist of fruits, madder, assafœtida, wool, and furs; in exchange for which they bring back cotton cloths, brocades, and muslins." In fact the *Kharotis* of Afghanistan still carry on the same trade which the *Kalustrii* of Gândhâra pursued four centuries before the Christian era.

In the Babylonian and Scythian versions of the inscription of Darius the name of *Parupamisana* is substituted for Gâdâra (or Gândhâra). The former would appear to have been the Persian name, while the latter was the Indian name. In the Bundahis, the Murgâb, the Hari-rud, and the Helmand are all said to have their sources in Mount *Apârsen*. Ptolemy also includes the upper course of the Kabul River. These accounts agree with the description of Strabo, that "the southern parts of the Paropamisus belong to Ariana and India, the northern parts toward the west to Bactriana." As Ptolemy excludes the district of Gandaritis, the Paropamisadæ may be described as embracing all the peoples of the *upper courses* of the Merv, Hari-rud, Helmand, and Kabul Rivers. Strabo also particularly notices that though "the Macedonians gave the name of Caucasus to all the mountains, yet among the barbarians the heights and the northern parts of the *Paropamisus* were called *Emoda* and Mount *Imaus;*" that is, the Indians called them *Himâvat*, or snowy mountains. The Paropamisadæ therefore corresponded with the mountainous districts in the upper sources of these rivers, which are now held by the mixed races called Hazâras.

Of the early inhabitants of the mountainous country we know absolutely nothing. Dionysius indeed mentions the *Satraïdæ* as dwelling πτυχὶ Παρπανισοῖο in the valleys of Paropamisus in common with the Ariani. Priscian retains the name (v. 1004) in his translation; but Avienus changes it to *Sagam infidum*, as if he considered them to be *Sacæ*. The name may, however, be compared with *Satraphernes*, *Sitraphernes*, *Sitratachmes*, and others derived from the *Chitra* or leopard. *Shetharboznai*, or in the Septuagint Σαθαρβουζαναί, is commonly found in the form of *Sati-barzanes*, just as *Chitra* has become *Chita* in the spoken language. Hence perhaps the *Sattraïdæ* may be the same people as the *Sattagudai* of Herodotus, and the *Thatagush* of Darius's inscriptions, whom some writers have identified with the Paropamisadæ.

But whoever may have been the first inhabitants of Paropamisus, it is certain that the earliest occupants of whom we have any clear mention are the Afghan tribes of *Ghor*, the Suri and Lodi, who were employed under Subuktagîn and Mahmud in the end of the tenth century A.D. The Hazâras are not mentioned until the time of Mangu Khan, who sent an army of Mugals to the assistance of Hulâku, about A.D. 1250. Abul Fazl says that the "tribe of Hazâra are the remains of this army," and that "they inhabit the country from Ghazni to Kandahar and Maidân, to the borders of Balkh." Utbi, the historian of Mahmud, speaks of Avghâns, Turks, and Khiljis. At a later date different writers speak of *Avghân* and *Jarmai* Hazâras. I agree with Sir William Jones and Dr. Dorn in considering the Afghans as the original inhabitants of the country, the Paropamisadæ of the time of Alexander.

It must be remembered that the peoples to the west of the Indus did not call themselves Afghans, that name having been applied to them by their Persian neighbours. Muhabbat Khan says, "The original spelling of this word is *Afghân*, but *fa* not being used in the Afghan language, I have placed it under the head of *alif* and *vau*." Accordingly he spells the name *Avghân*, with the plural *Avghâniân*. This is the form used by the Chinese pilgrim Hwen Thsang in A.D. 620, who, on leaving *Fa-la-na* (Bannu), passed through *O-po-kien* on his way to *Ho-si-na* or Ghazni. *Opokien* is rendered by Julien as *Avakan*.[9] Of course he must have passed through the district of the *Kharoti* Afghans on his way from Bannu to Ghazni.

With regard to the Afghan claim to be the descendants of the ten lost tribes of Israel, it may perhaps be sufficient to point out that Saul, the son of Kish (or Talut bin Kish), belonged to the tribe of Benjamin, which was not one of the ten that were carried into captivity. This

[9] Julien's *Hwen Thsang*, i. 265.

claim, of course, was never heard of until their conversion to Islâm. It must be remembered also that there is another quite different genealogy which traces the descent of the Sultâns of Ghor from the Turanian Zohâk, whose children took refuge in the hills of Bamian, and eventually settled in Ghor after the victory of Faridun. In this long list there is not a single Hebrew or even Muhammadan name until four generations preceding Shah Muizuddin Ghori, the conqueror of India. Even so late as the beginning of the eleventh century Mahmud of Ghazni gave his sister in marriage to *Malik Shâhu*, the chief of the Afghans of Zabulistan. He became the father of the notorious Salâr Masaud Ghâzi.

The language of the Afghans is called Pashtu, and is said to derive its name from the Pashtun or Pakhtun clan, whose country is called *Pakhtunkha*, the *Paktuike* of Herodotus. Whether Pashtu was the language of the Afghans in the time of Alexander we have no means of proving, as most of the names preserved by the Greeks seem to be purely Indian. Thus SOPHYTES is simply *Subhuti*, SISIKOPTUS is *Sasigupta*, the KOPHES R. is the Vedic *Kubha*, and the ARAKHOTUS R. is the *Saraswati* or Harakhaiti. It is certainly most probable that the language of the people was Pashtu. But it is quite impossible to believe that the people who elaborated the *Gandharian* or *Kharoshtri* alphabet could have been even half as wild and barbarous as the Paktyans of Herodotus and the Kalustrii of Ktesias. Their accounts might perhaps be accepted as descriptive of the wildest dwellers of the mountain tracts, while the inhabitants of the valleys of the Kabul, the Kuram, the Arachotus, and the Arghandab Rivers were comparatively civilised by their intercourse with their Indian neighbours. To them I would ascribe the adoption of the

Persepolitan architecture, and its transmission to India, where it took root and flourished, uninfluenced by the subsequent introduction of Greek architecture into the Kabul valley and West Panjâb. To them also I would ascribe the introduction of the sculptor's art, and the knowledge of coined money before the advent of Alexander. All of these they no doubt learned from the Persians. And we know absolutely that Taxila, or *Takshasila-nagara*, was a "city of hewn stone," that Omphis, the Raja of Taxila, presented Alexander with 80 talents of *coined silver*, and that a *statue of Hercules* was carried in front of the army of Porus in his battle with Alexander.

The eastern Alani, or Albani, whether they were Afghans or Massagetæ, would appear to have been a people of some consequence during the early centuries of the Christian era. In A.D. 53 the *Dahæ* and *Sacæ* suddenly invaded Parthia and forced Vologeses I. to retire. A few years later, in A.D. 58, the Hyrkanians revolted, and sent an embassy to Nero which, on its return in A.D. 62, was sent by order of Corbulo by way of the Persian Gulf to escape the Parthians. A peace had been made but it was soon broken, as in A.D. 75 the Alani Scythians being allowed to go through Hyrkania, made a sudden raid through the Caspian Gates into Media. Pakorus, the Satrap of Media, fled before them, and Tiridates, the King of Kawan, was defeated. Flushed with their successful fray, the Alani returned with much plunder to their own country.

From this account of their march through Hyrkania, I conclude that the Alani must have occupied the Western Paropamisus, or the hilly districts lying between Herat on the west and Ghazni on the east, that is the whole of Western Afghanistan, including the little-known district of Feroz-koh and Ghor. This position is in full accord with their subsequent history in the time of Sapor II. When the Romans declared war against Persia, the Sassanian king was on his north-eastern frontier engaged with the Chionitæ, the Albani, and the Segistani. Sapor at once made peace with them, and succeeded in engaging them as allies in his war with Rome; Ammianus, who saw all three at the siege of Amida, describes them as powerful and brave allies, who were of signal service in the reduction of Amida. The *Chionitæ* I have identified with the *Tokhari* or *Kushâns* of Kabul, and the *Segestani* are well known as the *Sakas* of *Sakastene* or Sistan; but who were the Albani? In another place Ammianus describes the *Alani* as Massagetæ, who extended far to the East, even, as he was told, to the Ganges, or, in other words, towards India. Clearly they seem to be the same as the Alani of Josephus, who in A.D. 75 passed through Hyrkania and ravaged Media.

It is of course possible, and perhaps even probable, that there may have been some confusion between the names of *Albani* and *Alauni* or *Alani*, and that the Eastern *Alani* had no real existence. But the existence of the Eastern *Albani* seems to rest upon very sure grounds: (1) We have Sophytes, King of Albania; and (2) the King of the Albani who accompanied Sapor II. to the siege of Amida.

We have a signal example of a name given through sheer mistake in the West *Indies*, but this is probably a very rare case. The transference of a name is common enough, as in the case of the *Pârsis* of Bombay and the Rohilla Afghans of Rohilkhand. Inearlier times we have *Sakastene*, named after its *Saka* conquerors; Zâbulistân after the Zâbuli or Jâwali White Huns, and the country of Shah Kitor after Kidâra, the King of the Kushâns.

So the country to the west of the Indus, having been occupied by the descendants of *Anu*, the *Anuwâns* or *Anwans*, it may have been called Anwânia or *Albania* after them.

Later Indo-Scythians.

GREAT KUSHÂNS.

In my previous accounts of the Indo-Scythians I have traced briefly the histories of the two great hordes of *Sakas* and *Kushâns*, from their first appearance on the Oxus in the second century B.C., down to their final settlements in the countries to the south of the Indian Caucasus. The *Sakas*, under a long line of Princes, or Satraps as they chose to style themselves, continued to hold the provinces on the Lower Indus, with the neighbouring districts of Surashtra and Mâlwa, until the close of the fourth century A.D., when they were subjected by the powerful Gupta kings of Northern India.

Of the early kings of the *Kushâns* we have numerous coins. Hermæus, the last of the Greek Princes of Northern India, came to terms with Kujula Kadphizes, the "King of the Kushâns," and their two names appear on different sides of the same coins. By the Chinese the Kushâns were called *Ta-Yue-ti*, or the "Great Lunar Race."[10] but their true name, as found in both inscriptions and coins, was *Kushân*. In India, however, they were more generally known as *Tushâras*, or *Tukhâras*, or "Snow-landers," the

[10] That is, if *Yue* be taken for the "moon." But I incline to take *yue-ti* or *Gweti*, the general name given by the Chinese to several of the Tartan races. And further, I think that as *Ta* means "great," the *Ta-Gweti* must be the *Massa-Getæ*.

Τόχαροι of Ptolemy, the *Tochari* of Pliny and Ammianus, and the *Tu-ho-lo* of the Chinese pilgrim Hwen Thsang.

Of the speech of the Kushâns we know nothing except the titles of *Shao* and *Shaonano Shao*, or "King" and "King of Kings," as all their inscriptions are recorded in the well-known language of India. As they were Tûrks their language must have been *Tûrki*; but, as they were ignorant of writing, they must have adopted one or both of the two alphabets of their Greek predecessors. These were the *Greek*, which was written from left to right, and the *Gandharian* or *Kharoshtri*, which was written from right to left. On a few of their earlier coins the Kushâns adopted the Greek title of **ΒΑΣΙΛΕΥΣ** and **ΒΑΣΙΛΕΥΣ ΒΑΣΙΛΕΩΝ ΣΩΤΗΡ ΜΕΓΑΣ**, but these were dropped during the reign of Kanishka, and the only trace of the Greek language that I have found on any of the Indo-Scythian coins is the title of *Strategasa*, or Στρατηγός, taken by Aspa-varma, the "General" of Azas.

According to the Chinese all the kings of the *Tuholo*, or Tochari, bore the title of *Shao-wu*, which is transliterated in Greek by **ΖΑΟΟΥ**, or *Zavu*, on the coins of Kozola Kadaphes, and in Gandharian letters by *Yaviia* on some and by *Yaüga* on others.[11] I take this to be the same title as **ÞΑΟ**, or *Shao*, on the coins of the later Kings Kanishka, Huvishka, and Vâsu-deva, and the *Shâhi* of the Indian inscriptions of Kanishka and Vâsu-deva. This title of *Shâhi* continued in use amongst their Indo-Scythian successors down to the time of Mahmud of

[11] In his *Catalogue of the Coins of the Scythic Kings of India*, Mr. Percy Gardner, p. 123, notes that this word was originally wrongly read as **ΖΑΘΟΥ**, but he omits to mention that the correction had already been made by me in the *Num. Chron.* for 1872, fourteen years before.

Ghazni, as Beruni calls his enemy "Anangpâl the *Shâhi*," and the Raja Tarangini styles *Trilochanpâl* "the last of the *Shâhi* kings." The name of *Kushân* also survived until the ninth century, as Ibn Khordâdbeh calls the Ruler of Mâwar-un-nahar, the "King of the Kushâns."

Hwen Thsang describes the language of the *Tu-ho-lo* as being somewhat different from that of other countries; but their alphabet he describes as consisting of "twenty-five letters, which were written horizontally from left to right.[12] The language of *Bamian* and *Kapisa*, he says, was slightly different, but that of *Tsaokuta*, of which Ghazni was the capital, was quite different.[13] The *Indian* letters he states were forty-seven in number. As this last statement is strictly accurate, I have some confidence in the correctness of his description of the *Tuholo* or Kushân alphabet as consisting of twenty-five letters which were written from left to right. As this direction of the writing excludes all Semitic alphabets we have only the Greek and the Indian alphabets left from which to choose. The choice is not doubtful, as we know that the Kushâns continued to use the Greek alphabet on their coins until the time of Hormazd II. of Persia, A.D. 300, who had married a daughter of the King of Kabul. As the Greek alphabet has twenty-four letters, the addition of Þ or *sh* completes the number of twenty-five assigned by Hwen Thsang to the alphabet of the Tochari or Kushâns.

On the earliest coins bearing the name of **BAZO ΔHO** or *Vâsu Deva*[14] the Greek legends show little

---

[12] Beal, *Siyuki*, i. p. 88. [13] Beal, i. p. 50, and ii. p. 283.

[14] I claim the discovery of the true reading of this name, which was read as *Baraoro* by Wilson (*Ar. Ant.* p. 377). Thomas at first disputed my reading, but he eventually gave in.

debasement excepting in the letters Z, H, and N. The H has become Ͱ and the N has become H, while the Z has changed to a form like the Indian figure २. But on the later coins, which bear the names of KANHÞKO and BAZO ΔHO, the letters A and Δ have become round, and are not easily distinguished from O. I have seen no late *gold* coins of Huvishka, although very corrupt *copper* coins bearing his name are common. I note that the coins which have the name of *Kaneshko*, ending in *ko*, all bear the peculiar symbol of Vâsu Deva's money, on which account I attribute them to the late period of the third century A.D., after the death of Vâsu Deva. On all these later coins there are Indian letters in the field, either single letters or monograms. The reverse types of all these *later Kushân* coins are confined to the figures of the seated goddess *Ardokhsho*, or Lakshmi, and the standing god *Oksho* or Siva with his Bull. The former type prevailed in the Kabul valley and was adopted by the Sassanian kings for their Bactrian coins; the latter type prevailed in the East, where it was adopted by the Gupta kings in the middle of the fourth century A.D., and eventually it formed the lasting types of the Kashmir coinage down to the Muhammadan conquest in the fourteenth century.

All these *Later Kushân* coins may be divided into two classes, which I will call Class A and Class B. They formed the money of the Kabul valley and the Panjâb from the time of Vâsu Deva's death, or about 180 or 200 A.D., down to the settlement of *Kidâra Shah*, or *Ki-to-lo*, in Gândhâra, about A.D. 425. *Ki-to-lo*, the King of the Great Kushâns, established his son in *Purushâwar*, or Peshâwar, and thus formed the kingdom of the *Little Yue-ti*, or Lesser Kushâns.

Class A comprises a numerous series of gold coins bearing the names of *Kanisha* or *Vâsu Deva* in Greek letters, but always accompanied by Indian letters in the field outside the King's spear. The *Obverse* is the same on all, namely, the King standing as on the coins of Vâsu Deva, but the reverses have the two different types of *Ardokhsho* or *Oksho.* As these two deities are the representatives of the Indian *Lakshmi* and *Siva* I think it probable that the coins may have been the produce of different places where the worship of *Vishnu* and *Siva* was respectively in favour. The greater number of these coins are found in the Panjâb, but a few gold coins have been found in Stûpas, in the Kabul valley. The *Lakshmi* coins are specially common in North-West India, while the *Siva* coins come principally from the West. The former belonged to the Eastern provinces, the latter to the Western provinces of the Kushân Empire.

Many years ago, after I had deciphered the title of *Strategasa* on the coins of Aspa Varma, the son of Indra Varma, the "general" of Azas,[15] I formed the opinion that these coins with Greek legends and Indian letters in the field might perhaps be the local issues of Indian mints under different satraps, whose names might be indicated by the Indian letters. These satraps might have been either Indo-Scythian nobles, or native chiefs, the tributary Hindu rulers of their ancestral dominions. We now know that *Yen-Kao-chin* or *Yen-Kao-chin-tai,* the son of *Kieu-tsieu-khio,* conquered India, and established his "*generals*" as governors in the name of the *Yueti* or *Kushâns.* This Prince *Yen,* or *Wen,* is the famous *Wema Kadphises* from whom all the chiefs of Bactria and Sogdiana claimed

---

[15] Published in the Bengal Asiatic Society's Journal for 1854.

descent.[16] The same system of Government was no doubt continued under his successors *Kanishka, Huvishka*, and *Vâsu-deva*, and was probably continued down to the close of the Kushân rule. Unfortunately the Indian letters on coins of this class are usually single characters, excepting in the three examples of *Viru, Mahi*, and *Vâsu*, which might represent genuine Hindu names, such as *Virudpaka, Mahidhara*, and *Vâsu-deva*. But though the names may be Indian, the men might have been Indo-Scythians; for we know that the son of *Chashtana* was *Jayadâma*, the son of *Râjubula* was *Sodâsa*, and the son of *Chhagaliga* was *Vishnu-dâsa*. In all these instances the *Scythian* father gave his son an *Indian* name. The fact is that the Kushâns themselves soon became *Hinduized*, and the *Scythian Huvishka* was followed by Bazo-deo or *Vâsu-deva*, whom I would identify with *Jushka*, of the Raja Tarangini. On his accession he probably took the Indian name. A barbarous race of conquerors settled amongst a more numerous and more civilised people soon loses its nationality. After the conquest of India and their conversion to Buddhism the Kushâns became thoroughly Hinduized, and gradually adopted the alphabet as well as the language of the conquered people. I have already remarked the prevailing use of Indian letters on the coins bearing the name of Vâsu Deva, as well as the entire absence of any inscriptions of his reign in Gândharian letters. The only Gândharian inscription of an undoubted later date is my stone record from Panjtâr, which is dated in s. 122, or A.D. 200.[17] It mentions the *Maharayasa Gushanasa Raja*

---

[16] *Yen, Wen*, and *Hen*, I understand to be different pronunciations of the same character.

[17] Bengal Asiatic Society's Journal, 1854, "Coins of Indian Buddhist Satraps."

. . . . but the name is unfortunately lost. As Vâsu Deva's earliest record is dated in S. 74, or A.D. 152, and his latest in S. 98, or A.D. 176, this Panjtâr inscription must almost certainly belong to some later king. I have read the date of a short inscription found by Mr. L. King, at Hashtnagar, as S. 274 or 275, equivalent to A.D. 352-53.[18] There is no objection to this later date, as we know from Samudra Gupta's Allahabad Pillar inscription that the *Daiva-putra Shâhân-Shâh* was his contemporary. As these are the titles of the Kushân kings it is certain that they were still powerful. The use of the Gândharian alphabet may still have lingered amongst the people, although it had been given up by the kings.

All the coins of the later Kushâns present the same uniform type of *Obverse* of the king standing to the front, with his right hand extended over a small altar, and holding in his left hand either a spear or a trident. The inscriptions on the early coins of Class A are all in debased Greek letters, which when nearly complete give the names and Kushân titles of Kanishka and Vâsu Deva. On the *Reverse* there are only the two well-known types of the seated goddess ΑΡΔΟΧÞΟ, and the standing god ΟΚÞΟ with his Bull. I notice that with the former type the king holds a spear or sceptre, but with the latter a trident.

The obverse legend is ÞΑΟΝΑΝΟ ÞΑΟ ΚΑΝΗÞΚΟ ΚΟÞΑΝΟ, or ÞΑΟΝΑΝΟ ÞΑΟ ΒΑΖΟΔΗΟ ΚΟÞΑΝΟ.

The reverse legend is either ΑΡΔΟΧÞΟ, or ΟΚÞΟ.

On all of them the symbol is uniformly that of Vâsu Deva.

---

[18] The date of 274, published by Mr. V. Smith, *Indian Antiquary*, 1889, p. 257, is not quite certain; but I still think it must be 274 = A.D. 352, and I see that Dr. Bühler accepts the reading of the date, but doubts whether it can be referred to the era of 78 A.D. The earlier era of 57 B.C. would give 217 A.D.

In Plate I. I have arranged all the early coins on which the principal monogram in Indian letters is placed outside the king's spear. On a few specimens there is only a single Indian letter; but on most of the coins there are Indian monograms or letters in three different parts of the field—(1) on the left, near the king's right foot; (2) in the middle, between the king's feet; (3) on the right, outside the king's spear or trident.

On these gold coins I think it probable that we have the names, in monogram, of some of the first successors of the great Kushân Princes, Kanishka, Huvishka, and Vâsu Deva. On some coins the names may perhaps be those of the satraps or governors of particular provinces. In this case I should expect to find the name of the province or city of the satrap, in addition to his name.

In the following table I have arranged all the Indian monograms and letters, showing their positions on the coins as left, middle, and right. In this way they can be more readily compared with each other.

Reverse, ΑΡΔΟΧÞΟ.

Pl. I. No.	King.	Obverse.			Reverse.
		Left.	Middle.	Right.	
1	Kanishka	—	—	Pa	
2	,,	Ha	—	Vi	
3	,,	Nya	Thâ	Vi	Thâ
4	,,	Nya	—	Viru	Ru
5	,,	Sa	Chu	Vâsu	
6	,,	Sa	Ga	Vâsu	
7	,,	Khu	Chhu	Vâsu	
8	,,	Bha	Ga	Vâsu	
9	,,	Vai	Thâ	Chhu	Thâ
10	,,	Vai	Thâ	Si	Thâ
11	,,	—	Pu	Mahi	
12	,,	—	—	Bhṛi	

Reverse, OKÞO

Pl. I. No.	King.	Obverse. Left.	Obverse. Middle.	Obverse. Right.	Reverse.
13	Vâsu Deva	—	—	Ha	Ha
14	,,	Raju	Gho	Rada	
15	,,	—	—	Pri	
16	Kanishka	Ga	Gho	Hu	
17	,,	Ha	Thâ	Auṁ	
18	,,	Ga	Gho	Phri	

Class B.—The coins of this class are chiefly of gold. Some of the copper specimens are undoubtedly ancient forgeries, from which the gilding has worn off. They still present the remains of Greek legends in the margin, but the letters are illegible, and seem to be a mere repetition of o o o. Indian letters now appear in two or three places of the field. One monogram occurs outside the king's spear, as before. A second monogram is under his arm, and a third is placed under his right hand, near the altar. In 1883 Mr. E. Thomas published a paper on this class of coins, in which he treated the monograms outside the spear as giving the names of different tribes of Scythians, while the letters under the king's arm he explained as the "names of kings or military chiefs located in India," apparently as independent rulers.[19]

During the past forty years I have made several attempts to read these monogram names, in much the same direction as Mr. Thomas. But, though our methods agree generally as to the names, I prefer to take the monograms

[19] *Indian Antiquary*, vol. xii. pp. 6—11.

outside the spear as indicating places, the seats of distinct Satrapies. So, also, I look upon the names under the arm as those of the Satraps, or governors of provinces tributary to the great Kushân Kings of Gândhâra. On the Gupta coins the kings' names are placed perpendicularly under the arm.

Mr. Thomas gives the names of five different tribes as:— 1. *Shaka.* 2. *Kushân.* 3. *Gaḍaha.* 4. *Shandhi.* 5. *Mahi.*

The readings of *Shâka* and *Kushân* are incontestable. *Gaḍaha* on well-preserved specimens is *Gaḍahara*, and on some of my coins I find *Gaḍakhara*, which is perhaps only a variant of the same name. The reading of *Shandhi* I cannot accept, as the monogram appears to begin with P, which *may be* followed by SH, but which is certainly followed by K, over which is placed the vowel I. Then come Ṇ and ḌH, which make up *Pakiṇḍha*, or *Pakaṇḍhi.* If the letter SH be admissible, then the name may be *Pashkiṇḍha*, or *Pushkaṇḍi.* But there still remains another element of doubt in the upright stroke which passes through the cerebral ṇ, which would add either H or L, or both, to the monogram. The name might, therefore, possibly be *Pakalahaḍhi*, or even *Pushkalaṇḍhi*, which would represent the Pakhali of the present day.

Mr. Thomas's MAHI is, of course, a correct reading, but I think the name must be that of a king, and not that of a tribe. I have, therefore, included my specimen of *Mahi* in Class A.

In proposing geographical names for these monograms, in preference to the tribal names advocated by Mr. Thomas, I am guided chiefly by the fact that all these coins are found in the Northern Panjâb, where we know that several districts were under the rule of satraps, or governors, who were appointed by the paramount sovereigns of Gândhâra. At present I cannot offer any absolute proofs of my proposed assignments, but they appear to me to be much more probable than those proposed by Mr. Thomas. The following are my proposed readings :—

I. Shâka.—Thomas has duly noted that this name is always spelt on the coins with the cerebral sibilant *sh*, ष instead of the palatal *ṣ*, श. But he has omitted to notice that the name on the coins is generally *Shâka* with the long *â*, which is never used for the name of the *Săka* tribe. I prefer, therefore, to read *Shâka* as intended for the city of *Shâkala*, which was the capital of the Eastern Panjâb. It was the residence of the Greek King Menander, and in later times of the Hûn King Mihirkul. It is the *Sangala* of Alexander's historians, the *Sâkala* of Ptolemy, the *Shâkalhâ* of the Chach-nâma, and the *Sangala wâlatiba* of the present day. Taking the monograms under the king's arm as the names of satraps or governors, I think that it is much more probable that there were six or eight rulers of Sangala, than that so many chiefs of the *Săka* tribe were employed under the Kushân kings.

II. Gaḍahara and Gaḍakhara.—I am not satisfied with the reading of the first half of the name as Gaḍa, although it has the support of Thomas. I notice that the first letter has a considerable upturn from its left member, and that the second letter may possibly be R with a turn to the left to connect it with a long *â* over the next letter H. I should like to read the whole name as *Nagarahâra*, if there was any authority for taking the *upturn stroke* before *g* as a connected *n*. *Nagarahâra* was the name of the ancient city near Jalâlâbâd, in the middle of the Kabul valley. It is the *Nagara* or *Dionysopolis* of Ptolemy; and one of these very coins was found by Masson in No. 10 Tope at Hidda close by, along with gold coins of Theodosius II., Marcian, and Leo.[20] The only king's name noted by Thomas is *Kiraḍa,* of whom I possess three specimens; but I have a single coin of a second king named *Peraya.* Of the *Gadakhara* or *Nagarahâra* type I have two coins with the name of SAMUDRA in full under the arm. This reading of *Nagarahâra* I offer with some hesitation as only tentative.

Thomas quotes the tribe of *Shaṇḍa* from the Mahâbhârata (*Ind. Ant.,* xii. 8); but they appear to be placed in the East, and I do not see how they could have struck coins in the Kabul valley. I think these Shaṇḍas may be identified with the Shandus of the Arrakan frontier, who are noted in the following paragraph :—

"The Shendus, on the northern frontier of the Arrakan hill tracts, have sent a challenge to Mr. Greenstreet, the Superintendent of Police at Akyab, to come out and fight; and no doubt (says an Indian paper) when that gentleman receives a reinforcement of the Karen levy, now on the way to Akyab, he will oblige them." (*Homeward Mail,* December, 1892.)

III. PAKAṆḌHI (the SHANDI of Thomas).—This name has already been discussed. It may possibly be the full name of the district of PAKHALI, to the north of Râwal Pindi.

Mr. Thomas's paper in the *Indian Antiquary* for 1883 deals chiefly with the coins of the Class B.[21] I have been able to add a few new names, Nos. 7, 9, and 11; and I have suggested a few different readings of some of the old names. On No. 13, for instance, I read *Bâshan* instead of *Bâsan,* as the sibilant is quite unmistakably the Gupta

---

[20] *Ariana Antiqua,* Pl. XVIII., 25.

[21] *Indian Antiquary,* vol. xii. p. 8.

sh. I utterly reject his reading of the title of *Shandhi* on Nos. 12 and 13, for reasons already stated. I also reject his explanation of the female figure of *Ardokhsho* on the reverse as the Indian "*Ardha-nâri,* or half-male and half-female figure of the androgyne Siva." The figure is unmistakably a female only, with two breasts, and the usual female costume. She is, in fact, the goddess *Lakshmi.* The following table describes the names on all the coins of this class that have come under my notice.

Reverse, ΑΡΔΟΧÞΟ.

Pl. II. No.	King.	Obverse.			Reverse.
		Left.	Middle, under arm.	Right.	
1	Mi	Khai	Mi	Shâka	
2	Sita	Bha	Sita	Shâka	
3	Bha or Bhu	Te	Bha	Shâka	
4	Bhṛi	—	Bhṛi	Shâka	
5	Saya, Salya	Bha	Saya	Shâka	
6	Saya, Salya	Bha	Saya	Shâka	
7	—	Bha	—	Shâka	
8	Pra	—	Pra	Shâka	
9	Peraya	Kapan	Peraya	Gaḍahara	Sha
10	Kirada	Kapan	Kirada	Gaḍahara	Ghasha } Yasha }
11	Samudra	Pu	Samudra	Gaḍahara	
12	Bhadra	—	Bhadra	Paḳalhdhi	
13	Báshan	Nu	Bâshan	Pakalhdhi	

The two seals shown in Plate III. certainly belong to the Kushâns of the second or third century A.D., as they have Indian letters on them as well as Indo-Scythian Greek characters. These characteristics distinctly associate them with the coins of Plate I. of the same date.

In A.D. 630 the Chinese pilgrim Hwen Thsang, after passing through Samarkand and Darband, reached the valley of the Oxus, which he describes as the country of the *Tu-ho-lo* or *Tokhari*, that is the Great Yuêti or *Kushâns*. Their language, he says, was slightly different from that of other peoples, while their alphabet consisted of twenty-five letters, which were written from left to right.[22] This is a very important statement, as it points distinctly to the use of the Greek alphabet. We know from numerous coins and inscriptions that the Kushâns used three different alphabets—the Gândharian, the Greek, and the Indian. The first of these is barred by being written from right to left, and the last is barred by the number of its letters which considerably exceed forty, while we know that it was not in use on the Oxus. This leaves only the Greek alphabet, which, excluding the *digamma* and the *koppa*, that were not used, and including the *sanpi*, or *sh* which was used by the Kushâns, consisted exactly of twenty-five letters, and was moreover written from left to right.

Some of the Indo-Scythic Greek characters have been much corrupted; but such as I have been able to recognise I have given at the bottom of the plate. Some of the letters are very little changed, as the **B** and **Z** in **BAZO** and in **BIZAΓO**. The **P** also retains its form, and is clearly distinguishable from **Þ** or *sh*. The **A** becomes gradually a simple **O**, and so also does the **Δ**. The letters **H** and **N** become confounded with each other. The vowel **Y** is used in the name of Huvishka on the *Sarapo* coin, Pl. XXIII. 8, in **OOYOHÞKO**, which I read as *Houveshko*. It is also used in the name of the god **ÞAYPHOPO**, Pl. XXII. 9, which I read as *Shau-Reoro*. Gradually it became the fashion to link some of the letters, as **KO** and **NO** in *Kaneshko* and in *Kushâno*. Several

[22] Beal's *Hwen Thsang*, i. 38.

other letters are also linked, but I have not succeeded in making them out satisfactorily. I shall refer to the subject again in my account of the coins of the Scytho-Sassanians.

No. 1. Crystal seal. 0·825 in. by 0·625 in.

Male bust, with moustache and earrings, looking to the right. The hair is not bound with a diadem; but, in spite of this want, I think that the head is a royal one, as the Indian inscription on the left reads distinctly, SHÂNE, "the King," while that on the right, in corrupt Greek characters, certainly begins with the letter Þ, or *sh*. I think that it may be read as *Sh · a · u · n · o*, or *Shahno*, being only a repetition of the Indian legend.

From this seal we get a direct proof that the abnormal letter Þ actually does represent the Sanskrit letter *Sh* of the Sanskrit. Dr. Stein had already shown this from the names of *Kanishka*, *Huvishka*, and *Kushân*, as well as from the word ÞAO being used as the equivalent of the Greek BACIΛEYC.

No. 2. Nicolo seal. 1·4 in. by 1·05.

The larger seal, a fine nicolo, represents an Indo-Scythian prince in a standing position, doing reverence to the Indian god Vishnu. The god, who is standing to the front, has four arms. In the lower right hand he holds a club, as *gadâ-dhar*, and in the upper right hand a discus, as *chakra-dhar*. The lower left hand rests on a wheel, and the upper left hand a flower, perhaps the lotus. He wears a crown, and the Indian *dhoti*, or waist-cloth, and has both bracelets and armlets.

On his right hand stands the king, who is only half the height of the god, with hands clasped in adoration. The head-dress of the Raja is a round jewelled helmet, similar to that worn by King Huvishka on several of his coins, with a crescent enclosing a dot on the side. (See *Ariana Antiqua*, Pl. XIII., figs. 2 and 9, and Prinsep's *Antiquities*, Pl. V., fig. 2, and Pl. XXIX., fig. 20.) In Plate I. I have given two specimens of these coins, No. 4, with reverse of **MAO**, and No. 5, with reverse of **MAACHNO**, with the same helmet. As a similar helmet is not worn by any of his successors, I feel inclined to assign this seal to Huvishka himself. This attribution is rendered probable by the fact that Huvishka had already published his devotion to the goddess **NANA** on the copper coin given in the plate as fig. 3.

The Indian letter between the figures I read as KHAI. A similar monogram name is seen on the coin, fig. 1 of Pl. II., with the letter MI under the arm, which is the position for the king's name. The coin is an early one, probably as early as 250 A.D.

The longer inscription, in corrupt Greek letters, to the right, I cannot read. But I see that it begins with **ΓΟΓΟ**, or **ΠοΠο**, in similar form to the same four characters on the Huvishka copper coin. The letter **Þ**, or SH occurs, and so does the **P**, or R, to show that the letters are Greek.

There are a few other seals which may be assigned to the same period. As they have already appeared in my plates, it will be sufficient to refer briefly to them.

Kushân Plate XXI. 16. Agate seal.

Female figure, with modius on head, and cornucopia in left hand, exactly like the *Ardokhsho* of the coins. Right hand extended towards a child. Greek legend, **ÞΟΟΓΑΟ** = *Shao-Gao* = Queen of the Earth.

Kushân Plate XXI. 15. Sardonyx seal.

Female figure, with modius on head, and cornucopia in left hand, as on the last. A lunar crescent above, and a child behind. ΧΑÞΟΒΑΛΑΝΟ, *Khâsho-Balano*,

Kushân Plate XXII. 18. Jacinth seal.

The goddess ΝΑΝΑ, sitting, to front, on a recumbent lion. ΦΡΕΙΧΟΔΑΝΟ.

Kushân Plate XXII. 18. Agate seal.

The goddess ΝΑΝΑ, seated, with crescent over head. Legend not read.

INDO-SCYTHIANS. LATER KUSHANS. PLATE I.

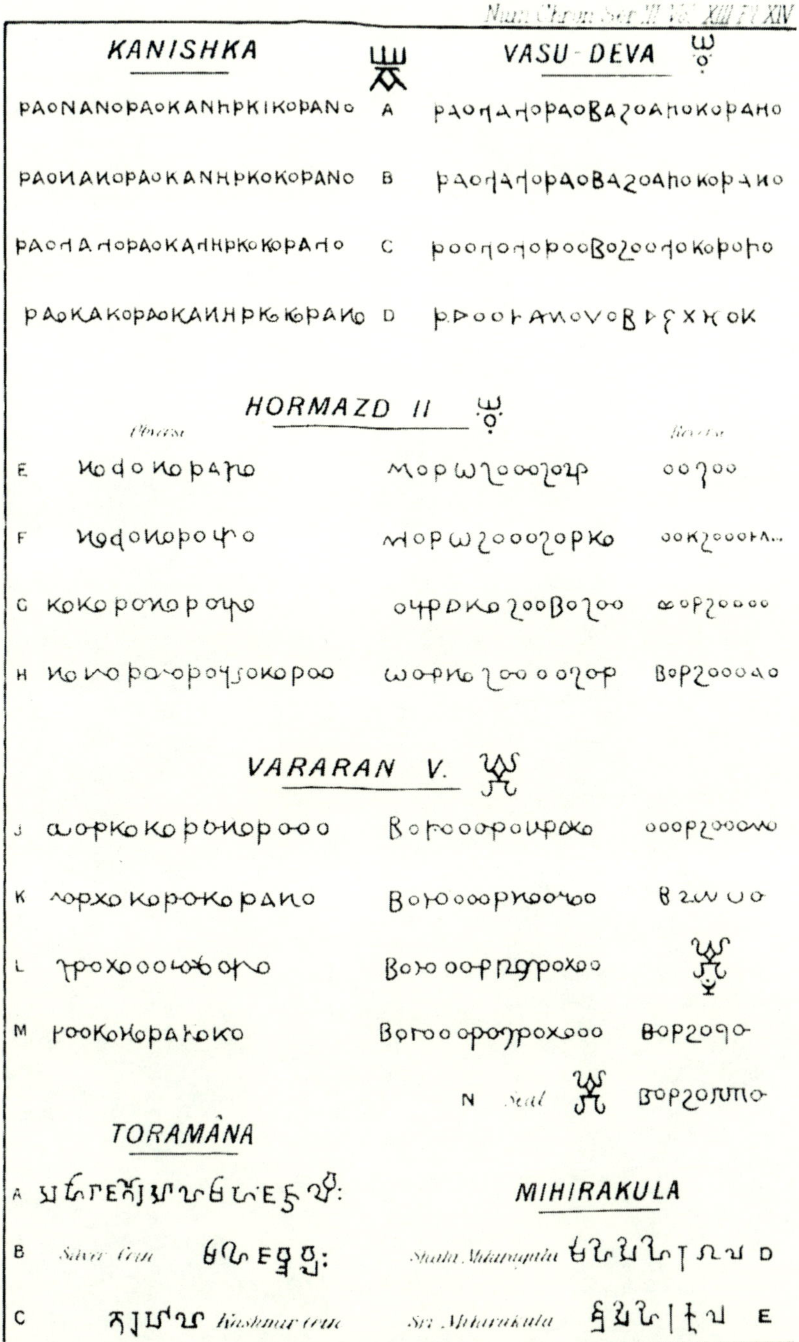

Pl V

SCYTHO SASSANIANS.

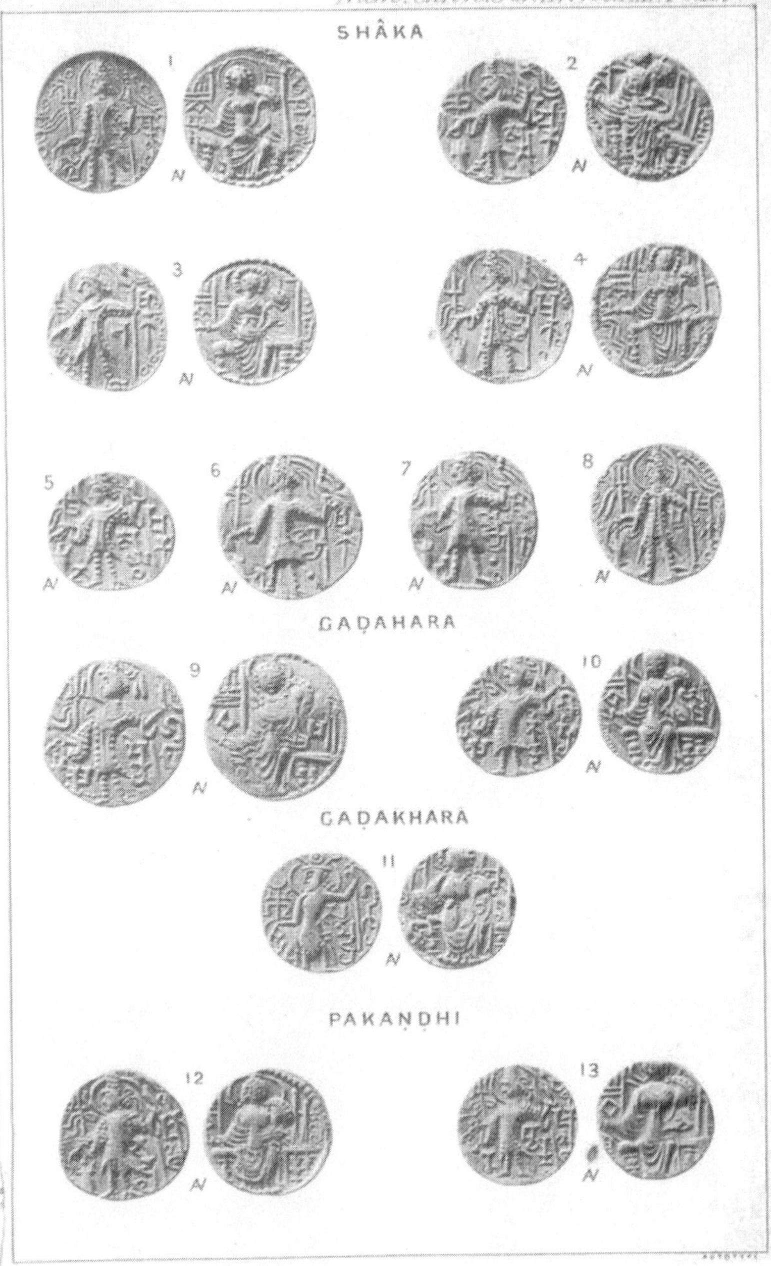

INDO-SCYTHIANS. LATER KUSHANS. PLATE II.

GREAT KUSHANS

PORTRAITS FROM SEALS & COINS (ENLARGED).

INDO-SCYTHIC GREEK ALPHABET.

Α	Δ Δ Δ Ο Ο	Ι	Ι Ι	Ρ	Ρ
Β	Β Β	Κ	Κ Κ Κ Κ Κο=κο	Σ	C
Γ	Γ Γ	Λ	Λ Λ	Τ	Τ
Δ	Δ Δ D Ο Χ	Μ	Μ Μ	Υ	V Υ Ϥ
Ε		Ν	Ν h Η Νο=νο	Φ	Φ
F		Ξ		Χ	
Ζ	Ζ ζ ζ ζ ζ	Ο	Ο Ο	Ψ	
Η	Η Η Κ	Π	Π	Ϻ	Þ
Θ	Θ	Ϙ		Ω	ω ω ω

INDO-SCYTHIANS. LATER KUSHANS. PLATE III.

LATER INDO-SCYTHIANS,

SCYTHO - SASSANIANS

AND

LITTLE KUSHÂNS.

BY

MAJOR-GENERAL SIR A. CUNNINGHAM, R.E.,
K.C.I.E., C.S.I.

REPRINTED FROM THE NUMISMATIC CHRONICLE,
VOL. XIII., SER. III., PAGES 166—202.

LONDON:
1893.

LATER INDO-SCYTHIANS.

SCYTHO-SASSANIANS.

(See Plates XIII., XIV.)

THE coins which I am now about to describe have been known for the last fifty years by the name of "*Indo-Sassanian.*" I prefer the name of "*Scytho-Sassanian,*" as being more correctly descriptive of the Sassanian costume of the kings with their peculiar Sassanian symbols. The earliest notice of them is by James Prinsep, who examined the specimens obtained by Kerâmat Ali, the companion of Arthur Conolly.[1] He recognised that the inscriptions were in corrupt Greek characters, in which all the vowels were represented by **O**, which in Pahlavi is used for the inherent short *a* of Devanâgari. A few years later Wilson described them as large and convex pieces, with the inscription a mere circle of **O**'s occasionally varied with **P**. He notes that, although found in the Kabul valley, these coins are "most plentifully met with in Badakshân," where Dr. Lord was informed that they were believed "to belong to a race of Rajput Princes once sovereigns of the province." The large coin with the ram's horns on the king's head-dress (Pl. IV., Fig. 15) is specially noted as having been found in Badakshân; and

---

[1] *Prinsep's Antiquities*, by Thomas, i. 129.

another coin equally large, with a plume surmounting the head-dress (*A. A.* xiv. 16) was obtained at Kunduz.[2]

Wilson further notes that several specimens were in the possession of Dr. Swiney, and that others had been sent to England by Dr. Lord and Sir Alex. Burnes. As I am aware that Dr. Swiney's collection was purchased from Kerâmat Ali, the fellow-traveller of Arthur Conolly, the specimens seen by Wilson were doubtless the same as those previously described by Prinsep. We thus learn that this collection came from the same country as the later acquisitions of Lord and Burnes, that is from Badakshân and Kunduz, or the districts on the Oxus, to the north of the Hindu Kush.

Having discovered the country to which these coins belong, the next step is to ascertain their date. On examination we see that the earliest specimens are very close imitations of the later, or posthumous, coins of the Kushân king, Vâsu Deva. The early money of this prince consists of pieces of gold, from 120 to 124 grains in weight, rather less than one inch in diameter, and of about the same thickness as an English sovereign. His later money gradually becomes thinner and broader, with a slightly convex obverse, while the Greek legend becomes more corrupt. The true name of the king was first read by myself as BAZO ΔHO, the Greek form of *Vâsu Deva*, or *Bâs Deo*, whose inscriptions I saw dug up at Mathura in 1861. Of the early coins, three of which were found in a stûpa at Ali Masjid, the legend is (Pl. V., A and B),

ÞAONANO ÞAO BAZO ΔHO KOÞANO,
Shaonano Shao Bazo Deo Koshano.

Ariana Antiqua, pp. 378—379.

This soon became corrupted to (Pl. V., C),

ÞOOHOHO ÞOO BOZO OHO KOÞOHO,
Shoonono Shoo Bozo Deo Koshono.

Wilson read the name as *Baraoro*, but he had detected that the character following **BO** was something like the figure of the Sanskrit numeral for 2.[3] It was, in fact, the badly formed **Z** of **BOZO**.

On all the later coins which retain the name of **BAZO ΔHO**, or simply **BAZ ΔHO**, however much corrupted, the king's head-dress remains unchanged as a conical helmet or tiara, apparently covered with rows of jewels. But on all the thin, broad convex pieces, which I call Scytho-Sassanian,' the head-dress assumes a decidedly Sassanian character. The same titles of *Shaonano Shao Koshano* are retained, but the name of *Bazo Deo* is gone, and a different name follows *Koshano*. On the reverse also there appears a second legend beside the old type of Siva with his bull Nandi. See the legends in Plate V. under the name of Hormazd II., Figs. E, F, G, H. At first the usual adjuncts of the original old type were retained, namely the *Triratna* Buddhist symbol on the right, and the *Swastika* between the king's feet.

Gradually the coins become larger and more convex, and the Greek legend more corrupt, while the obverse type of the king standing by an altar, and the reverse type of Siva and his bull Nandi, remain the same but of ruder execution. Various changes appear in the king's head-dress, such as a lion's head with open mouth on the front of the helmet, a round tiara surmounted by a tall plume, a helmet with a pair of ram's horns. On all these coins of Sassanian appearance the dress of the king

---

[3] *Ariana Antiqua*, p. 378.

approaches very closely to the well-known royal costume of the Sassanians. The trousers are now much fuller, the hair is much more bushy, while the ends of the diadem have become very broad, floating streamers, as seen on all the Sassanian coins.

These changes in the head-dress are of special importance in connecting these later coins with the Sassanian princes. Thus the *helmet* surmounted by a lion's head with open mouth is found upon several coins of the Sassanian king, Hormazd II., who reigned from A.D. 301 to 310. On a few of these he is styled king of the Kushâns (*Kushân malkân malkâ*).[4] The tall *Plume* type is copied from the portrait of *Pâpek Malkâ*, the progenitor of the Sassanians.[5] The *Ram's horns* are connected with Sapor II., who is described by Ammianus, on his advance against Amida, as "wearing, instead of a crown, a golden figure of a *Ram's head* inlaid with jewels."[6]

The only other coins of this class that I have met with are so extremely corrupt and barbarous that they show most decisively the decline of the Sassanian power in the country where they are found.

The extreme period which can be assigned to these coins may be about a century and a half, or from A.D. 300 to 450. The former date marks the accession of Hormazd II., who married the daughter of the Kushân king of Kâbul. The latter date marks the period when the White Huns, after a nine years' war with Isdegerd II.,

---

[4] See Plate IV., Fig. 2, a gold coin of Hormazd II. Brit. Mus. and Author.

[5] See Plate IV., Fig. 1, a silver coin of Ardeshir I., with Pâpek's head on the reverse. This coin is from General Court's collection.

[6] See Plate IV., Fig. 15, gold coin. Author.

became the dominant power on the Oxus. The earlier Sassanian princes were too much engaged with Rome and Armenia to find time for Eastern expeditions. But Varahrân II. obtained the title of *Segân Shâh*, or Σεγεστανῶν Βασιλεύς, by his conquest of Sakastene or *Segistan*, the country of the Sakas. The coins with the ram's horns on the head-dress bear the name of *Varahrân*, and might perhaps be assigned to this prince, as we know that he was on his Eastern frontier in A.D. 285, when the Emperor Carus invaded Persia. But as this Eastern expedition most probably refers to Sakastene or Sistan, and not to the countries on the Oxus where the coins are found, I would rather assign the coins to Varahrân V. or Bahrâm Gor, who defeated the White Huns near Merv, and appointed his brother Narses governor of Khorasân, with his capital at Balkh.

The coins of Hormazd II. were first assigned to this prince by E. Thomas, on the authority of a small copper piece with the figures of Siva and his bull, which gives the name of *Auhrmazd* in Pahlavi, with the title of *Laba-Kushân Malkân Malkâ*. A gold coin of the same king with a lion's head as a crest, but with the usual fire-altar and attendants on the reverse, bears the same inscription. Dr. Mordtmann disputes Thomas's reading, and proposes *bagi rushân* for *labâ-kushân*.[7] I possess a duplicate of the gold coin, and I unhesitatingly adopt Thomas's reading, but not his translation of "Lion-killer." My objection to his translation is chiefly based on the fact that, as Hormazd had married the daughter of the Kushân king,[8]

---

[7] *Num. Chron.*, xv., p. 182, and Pl. Fig. 8; Prinsep's *Indian Antiquities*, ii. 165; *Num. Chron.*, second series, xii. 38.

[8] *Khondemir*, Rehatsek's translation, ii. 340.

the title of *Kushân malkân malkâ* must refer to the Kushân alliance. But I object also to the hybrid *Labâ-Kushân* as not Persian. The well-known Persian term for a "lion-killer" is *Sher-afkan.* Strangely enough this title was given to the first husband of the celebrated *Nûr Jahân,* and was afterwards given to Nur Jahân herself by one of the courtiers of her second husband, the Emperor Jahangir, after she had killed four tigers with a musket. *Zani-sher-afkan,* he called her, which might either mean "Wife of Sher-afkan," or the "lady lion-killer."[9]

E. Thomas supposes that the lord of Kâbul may have been conquered by the Sassanian king, or have ceded a province to him. I would rather suggest that the King of Kâbul may have made peace with the Sassanian king by giving him a daughter and ceding the province of Balkh, to the north of the Hindu Kush. That the name of Kushân on the coins refers to the people appears to me to be absolutely certain, as it only repeats in Pahlavi what is recorded in corrupt Greek on the large thin gold coins with the figure of Siva on the reverse. On these coins the legend is simply (Pl. V., Hormazd II.)

ÞOONONO ÞOO KOÞONO, *Shaonano Shao Koshano*

on the left side, and on the right side some very corrupt Greek letters which may be read as ΟΥΡΟΜΑΖΔΟ ΒΑΓΟ.

The connection thus formed between the Persians and the Kushâns would seem to have been interrupted after some time, as Ammianus relates that when war broke out with Rome Sapor II. was lying in winter quarters on the borders of the *Chionitæ* and Euseni, with whom he at once

---

[9] Blochmann's *Ain Akbari*, p. 525, note 394.

made a treaty and returned to his own country.[10] Afterwards, in A.D. 358, at the siege of Amida, Sapor was accompanied by the kings of the Chionitæ and the Albani, of equal rank and splendour. *Grumbates*, the king of the Chionitæ, was "of middle age and wrinkled limbs, but of a grand spirit, and already distinguished for many victories." In the disposition of the troops of his allies no mention is made of the Euseni; but the four sides of the city are beleaguered by the *Chionitæ*, the *Albani*, the *Vertæ*, and the *Segestani*.[11] It seems certain that all were tribes from the north-eastern quarter of the empire. The *Segestani* we know are the *Sakas* of Sistan. The Chionitæ I take to be the Kushâns or Tokhari, as their name would seem to be only a literal Greek translation of the "snowmen" or *Tukhâras*, being regularly formed from χιών, "snow." They were therefore the people of Kabul and Balkh. The *Albani* might therefore be the people of the Paropamisus, the *Aoghâns* or *Eastern Albani*, or, perhaps, the inhabitants of *Labus* or *Elburz*, that is of Khorasân. The Caspian Gates were also called *Albaniæ Portæ*, because they led to the Eastern Albani. Polybius uses the term Λάβος or Δαβοῦτας for Elburz. *Laba-Kushân* may, therefore, mean simply the Kushâns of Elburz or Khorasân.[12]

It must be remembered that Prince Hormazd (the uncle of Hormazd II.), during the reign of his brother Narses, had sought refuge with the Scythians: "Ipsos Persas ipsumque regem adscitis *Saccis*, et *Russis*, et *Gellis*, petit frater Ormies," are the words of the Panegyric quoted by Gibbon. The first people are certainly the

---

[10] *Ammianus Marcellinus*, xvi. 9—4 and xvii. 5—1.

[11] *Ibid.* xviii. 6—1 and xix. 2—3.

[12] *Polybius*, x. 4.

Sacæ or *Sakas*; the second may be the *Euseni* of Ammianus, and the last may be his *Gelani*. Before his accession, therefore, Hormazd II. had already been on friendly terms with the Scythian tribes on his north-east frontier. The presence of his successor, Sapor II., upon the same frontier was no doubt necessary for the maintenance of his authority in that quarter. The only coins of Sapor that I can assign to his eastern dominion are the copper pieces (Plate IV., Fig. 9) with the corrupt Greek legend ÞΟΒΟΡΟ, *Shoboro,* of which I possess several specimens.

These provinces on the north-east frontier of Persia, which I believe to have been acquired by Hormazd II., and successfully held by Sapor II., must have been still in the possession of the Sassanian kings, when about A.D. 435 the king of the Ephthalites or White Huns suddenly crossed the Oxus and overran the province of Merv, or Margiana. The Sassanian king, Varahrân V., or Bahram Gor, at once took the field, and having twice defeated the Huns, he set up a pillar to mark his boundary, and appointed his brother Narses Governor of Khorasân, with Balkh as his headquarters.[13] It is to Bahram Gor, or Varahrân V., that I would assign the thin gold coins with the ram's horns, as they bear the peculiar symbol which is found on the known coins and seals of that prince.

In the reign of Bahram's successor, Isdegerd II., the White Huns again made a raid on the Sassanian territories. The Persian king, in A.D. 443, took up his residence at Nishapur and directed the war for nine years, until in A.D. 451 he crossed the Oxus and signally defeated them. Three or four years later, or about A.D. 455, the White Huns again invaded Khorasân. Isdegerd once

[13] Geo. Rawlinson, *Seventh Oriental Monarchy*, p. 298.

more drove them back, but, on following them across the Oxus, he fell into an ambush and was forced to retreat to his own territory. The Ephthalite king who was then reigning was *Chu-Khan*, the *Konkha* of Priscus. A fèw years later, from A.D. 464 to 485, during the reign of the Khâkân *Shulo-Puchin*, the *Khush Nawâz* of the Muhammadan historians, the White Huns renewed their raids, and the provinces to the south of the Oxus were permanently lost to the Persian kingdom.

Perhaps it may be objected to my attribution of these coins to the Sassanian kings that they may have been issued by the later Kushân kings of Kâbul in Sassanian costumes. But the fact that not a single specimen of these thin broad pieces has been found in any of the Stûpas of the Kâbul valley, offers a strong objection to their issue by any of the Kushân kings. The head-dresses also are exact copies of those worn by some of the actual Sassanian kings with their names given in Pahlavi characters. In the case of Varahrân I find the peculiar symbol which is used on most of his coins repeated on two different seals, one of which bears the name of the Sassanian king in Pahlavi characters.

We have also the strong evidence of the gold coins which are actually found in the Kâbul valley. They continue the costume of Vâsu Deva, with the addition of single Indian letters in the field.

The inscriptions in corrupt Greek as I read them are fully supported by the costumes of the kings; thus—

ΟΥΡΟΜΑΖΔΟ has the Lion's head as a crest, as on the Pahlavi coins of *Hormazd* II.

ÞΟ8ΟΡΟ has the turreted crown as on most of the coins of *Shahpur* II.

ΟΟΡΟΟΡΑΝΟ has the ram's horns as on the Pahlavi coins of *Varahrân* V.

Notes on the Coins.

In the corrupt Greek legends of these coins it will be seen that both the letters Α and Δ have become Ο, and that Ν and Η have assumed new forms as Ꮧ and Ⱶ, which are often used wrongly one for the other. The peculiar letter Ϸ = SH, the Β and the Ρ have alone remained unchanged. A comparison of the large gold coins will show that one-half of the legend comprising the royal title of "king of kings of the Kushâns" has been continued, more or less imperfectly, on all of them. But as the other half of the legend shows no trace of the name of *Bazo Deo*, it is clear that the rude characters must represent some other names.

Thus the coins with the Lion's head, which I attribute to *Hormazd* II., bear a legend in corrupt Greek characters as shown in Pl. V., Figs. E, F, G, H. The last gives the titles as *nano Shao Koshono Shao* on the left, and *Hoormozdo Oogor* on the right. Fig. G gives the name as *Ouramozdo Bogor*. The term *Bogor* I take to be intended for *Bagpur* or *Bagaputra*, the *Devaputra* of India.[14]

The coins of *Shahpur* are unfortunately limited to copper, but the name in corrupt Greek is clearly ϷΟΒΟΡΟ, *Shoboro*. The king's name is written Σαβώρ by Syncellus, and *Schabour* by D'Herbelot, the Ρ in Persian words being frequently changed to Β, as in Badshah for Padshah.

The gold coins of *Varahrân* V., with Greek legends, offer two different head-dresses, both of which are found

---

[14] I note as a curious fact that the great Kushân kings Kánishka, Huvishka, and Vâsu Deva, in spite of their adoption of Zoroastrian deities, make use of the title of *Devaputra*, although *Deva* meant only *Demon* in Persia. Similarly Gondophares and his family are all *Devaputra*.

on the small copper pieces with Pahlavi legends. The attribution therefore seems certain, more particularly as it is supported by the evidence of a seal (Pl. V., Fig. N) with the head of *Varahrân* and his name in Pahlavi, accompanied by the peculiar symbol which is found on these gold coins. I have given four examples of the corrupt Greek legends (Pl. V., Figs. J, K, L, M), which I read as *Bogo Oorohrano,* for *Baga Varahrân.* The title on the coin with the ram's horns reads *Roononoka Kosho(no).* For the ram's horn head-dress I may quote the description given by Ammianus of Sapor II., as a "Ram's head inlaid with jewels," when the historian saw him as he advanced against Amida.

The legends on the reverse of these gold coins are written in the same corrupt Greek characters; but instead of the one short word *oksho* as on the Vâsu Deva coins, there are two distinct legends, of which the shorter one may be intended for *oksho.* The longer one seems to be *Borzono,* or something similar, on all the coins both of Hormazd and of Varahrân. It is possible that it might be intended for *Borzo Deo* for *Vâsu Deva,* which might have been considered as a general term for a king. The same legend is found on the seal (Pl. V. N.), with the symbol of Varahrân. On the coins of the later *Vâsu Deva* of Multân the name is similarly represented in Pahlavi by *Varsu Tef.* Hitherto we have not found any successor of the Kushân king Bazo Deo, and I think it quite possible that *Vâsu Deva* was considered to be the general term for the king of the Kushâns. In this view the name placed on the coins might be taken to denote a "vassal king," like Grumbates, king of the Chionitæ, who accompanied Sapor II. to the siege of Amida.

At this very time, A.D. 358, the Kushâns were still in

the height of their power, as the Samudra Gupta inscription on the Allahabad pillar mentions the presents sent by the *Devaputra Shâhi Shahânshâhi* to the Indian king. As these were the peculiar titles assumed by the great Kushân kings, the presents must have been sent by one of them. As Grumbates was still an active man at the siege of Amida in A.D. 358, and as Samudra Gupta's reign must have extended from about 345 to 380 A.D., he may himself have sent the presents to the great Gupta king. I am inclined to assign the coins Plate II., Fig. 6, of the Later Great Kushâns, with **GR** under the king's arm, to Grumbates.

The power of the Kushân kings in the beginning of the fourth century A.D., is shown by the costly presents and the splendour of the escort which accompanied the Kushân princess to become the queen of Hormisdas II. (A.D. 301 to 309).' It is possible that the lady may have been an aunt, or perhaps even a younger sister, of Grumbates.

DESCRIPTION OF THE PLATE.

No.	Metal.	Inches.	Grains.		Plate.
				[Author, unique.]	
1	Æ	0·80	55	Side-face of King Pâpak to left, with peculiar plume surmounting helmet. Pahlavi legend, *Bari bagi Pâpaki Malkâ.* I have given this coin for the sake of the tall plume on the helmet, which is imitated on the coins of Hormazd II. and Varahrân V. The obverse bears the head of his son, *Artashatr malkân malka*, exactly as published by E. Thomas.	IV. 1
				[Brit. Mus., Dupl. Author.]	
2	*N*	0·75	111	Bust of King to right, with Lion's head and tall plume in head-dress. Pahlavi legend, *Mazdisn bagi Auharmazdi Labâ Kushân Malkân Malkâ.* "The Mazdean divine Hormazd, of the *Labâ-Kushâns* king of kings." Fire altar with standing attendants. Pahlavi legend, the same as on the obverse, with the addition of *Malki* over the fire-altar. [See E. Thomas in *Num. Chron.* xv. 182.]	IV. 2
				[Brit. Mus., Author.]	
3	*N*	0·80	111	Full-length figure of King, with Lion's head and plume as in	IV. 3

DESCRIPTION OF THE PLATE—*continued.*

No.	Metal.	Inches.	Grains.		Plate.
				No. 2, holding trident in left hand, and pointing downwards to a small altar with right hand. Trident over altar. The combined *Tri-ratna* and *Dharma-Chakra* symbol to right, and *Swastika* between feet. Legend in corrupt Greek : ΝΟΝΟ ÞΑΟ ΚΟÞΟΝΟ ΟΥΡΟΜΑΖΟΟ ΒΑΓΟΟ, which appears to be intended for— ÞΑΟ ΝΟΝΟ ÞΑΟ ΚΟÞΑΝΟ ΟΥΡΑΜΑΖΔΟ ΒΑΓΟ, "The king of kings of the Kushâns, Hormazd the divine." Siva standing before the bull Nandi. [Author, duplicate.]	
4	*N*	1·10	72·5	King standing as on No. 3, with Lion's head and tall plume, the broad ends of diadem floating upwards behind head. Tridents and symbols as on No. 3, with three dots under left arm. Pahlavi legend as No. 3. Some of the characters vary slightly on different specimens, but they are clearly intended to represent the same legend. The Indian god Siva standing before the bull Nandi, with trident in left hand and noose in right hand. Pahlavi legend, varying, ΟΟΑΖΟΟΟΗΛΟΟ to right, and ϩΟSΟ to left. The last four letters are probably intended for ΟΚÞΟ written inversely.	

No.	Metal	Size	Weight	Description	Plate
				[Author.]	
5	AV	1·10	66·5	King standing as on last, with Lion's head and nimbus, but without plume (see *Ariana Antiqua*, xiv. 17). Pahlavi legend varying slightly from No. 4. The Indian god Siva with Bull, as on No. 4. Pahlavi legend, **OOP⅂ OOOHOOO.** No. 5 was a small gold coin of the same types as No. 4. (Author—now lost.)	IV. 4
				[Brit. Mus.]	
6	Æ	0·60	38·5	Bust of King as on No. 2. Pahlavi legend, *Auhramazdi Labâ-Kushân Malka*, "Hormazd of the Labâ-Kushâns King." (See E. Thomas in *Num. Chron.* xv. 184.)	IV. 6
				[Author, unique.]	
7	Æ	0·60	32	Bust of King, with Lion's head and plume. Pahlavi legend, *Auhramazdi* (*Malkâ*). Fire-altar, with bust and arms of human figure on top.	IV. 7
8	Æ	0·70	72·5	Bust of King, with Lion's head and plume. Pahlavi legend, *Auharmazdi Malkâ.* Fire-altar without attendants.	IV. 8
				[*Ar. Ant.* xvii. 13, 14.]	
9	Æ	0·75	72	Bust of King, with turreted crown surmounted by jewelled dome, bushy hair and beard, and broad fillets of diadem behind. Corrupt Greek, **ÞOBOPO**, which I read as	IV. 9

DESCRIPTION OF THE PLATE—*continued.*

No.	Metal.	Inches.	Grains.		Plate.
				Shaboro, for Shahpur II. The head-dress is certainly his. His name is written Σαβώρ by Syncellus, and *Schabour* by D'Herbelot. In fact, the Persian *p* is frequently pronounced *b*, as in *Badshah* for *Padshah*. Fire-altar, with *taurus* symbol on pedestal.	
10	—	—	—	Gem, with name of Varahrân—King's "Antique Gems," Vol. II., Pl. IV., 9.	IV. 10
11	—	—	—	Amethyst, with symbol of Varahrân and **8OPO2OJUſm** (General Pearse). [Author.]	IV. 11
12	AV	1·25	121·5	Full-length figure of King, with broad tiara surmounted by plume, two tridents, Tri-ratna symbol, and swastika. Three dots under left arm. Corrupt Greek legend: **ÞOONONO ÞAO KOÞONO BOΓO OOPOHOPOOO,** which I read as, *Shaonano Shao Kushano Bago Oorohorono,* "The king of kings of the Kushâns, divine Varahrân." The Indian god Siva, with his Bull, trident and noose. Corrupt Greek legend, **OOP2 OOAMOϽO** to right, and **O2 Oq** to left. Perhaps the former may be intended for *Oorhoorano*, and the latter for **OKÞO** or *Oksho*.	IV. 12

KIDÂRA SHÂHI

LITTLE KUSHÂNS. PL. VI.

SCYTHO-SASSANIANS. PL. IV.

				[Author.]	
13	AV	1·30	106	*Full-length figure of King*, as on No. 12, but symbol on right similar to that of Varahrân V., as used on his other coins and seals. Swastika omitted between feet. Corrupt Greek legend only slightly different from No. 12. The *Indian god Siva, with Bull*, corrupt Greek legend double struck.	IV. 13
				[Author, not shown.]	
14	Æ	0·60	29	*Bust of King*, with same headdress as on the gold coins Nos. 12 and 13. Pahlavi legend, *Varahrân Malkâ*. *Fire-altar*, with bust of man above. Legend lost.	
				[Author, unique.]	
15	AV	1·30	121	*Full-length figure of King*, as on Nos. 12 and 13, but with headdress surmounted by ram's horns and plume. To right, the *Varahrân* symbol and swastika. Corrupt Greek legend only a slight variant from No. 12. *Siva and Bull*, with corrupt Greek legend as on No. 12.	IV. 15
				[2 specimens, Author.]	
16	Æ	0·55	23	Bust of King, with ram's horns, and plume headdress, as on No. 15. Pahlavi legend, *Varahrân Malkâ*. *Fire-altar*, with male bust above, as on No. 7.	IV. 16, 17

Plate V.

A B C D (*left hand*) inscriptions on gold coins of *Kanishka*, with the symbol of Vâsu Deva, instead of his usual one. Probably posthumous coins, with corrupt Greek legends.

A B C D (*right hand*) inscriptions on coins of *Vâsu Deva*, with corrupt Greek legends, probably of late date and posthumous.

E F G H, inscriptions on large thin gold coins of Hormazd II. The King's dress is Sassanian and his helmet is surmounted by a lion's head, as on the gold coin, with his name in Pahlavi (Pl. IV., No. 2). It will be seen that the name is omitted between *Shaonano Shao* and *Koshano*, and a new name is given following *Koshano*. This I venture to read as *Ouromazdo* on one coin and *Hormazdo* on a second coin, followed by *Bazoo*, which may be intended for *Bago*, the "divine." The short legend on the reverse seems to read *Borzo*, for *Bago* or *Vâsu*, as we learn from the later coins of *Vâsu Deva*, king of Multân, whose name is written *Varsu Tef* in Pahlavi.

J K L M, inscriptions on large thin gold coins of *Varahrân* V. These legends are very corrupt. On J, I read ++ *nono sho koshono* followed by *Borooron bako*. The others give only slight variations for this reading.

N, is an amethyst seal belonging to General Pearse. It bears the same symbol which is found on the coin L, and on the known coin of *Varahrân* V. with the ram's horn (Pl. IV., Fig. 15).

The names of *Toramâna* and *Mihirakula*, at the foot of the Plate, will be referred to in my paper on "The White Huns," which forms Part IV. of the present series of "Coins of the Later Indo-Scythians."

LATER INDO-SCYTHIANS.

LITTLE KUSHÂNS.

(See Plate XV.)

THE coins of the Little Kushâns are of considerable interest, as they begin with **KIDARA** or **KI-TO-LO**, the *Shâhi* of the *Ta-Yueti*, or Great Kushâns, who founded the kingdom of the Little Yueti in Gandhâra about A.D. 425 to 430. In a previous brief account of this kingdom I have given my reasons for identifying *Kidâra* of the coins with the *Kitolo* of the Chinese writers, who conquered Gandhâra, and placed his son in the government of Peshâwar, while he returned to the westward to repel an inroad of the White Huns. I possess several gold coins and three silver coins of *Kidâra*. The former present the well-known types of the Kushân kings, with the standing raja and the sitting goddess; but the latter are of Sassanian type, giving the king's portrait in full face with his name, title, and tribe in Indian letters. The legend is *Kidâra Kushâna shâhi*, or "Kidâra king of the Kushâns." The reverse has the Sassanian fire-altar, with three letters or numerals on the base, and the usual attendant priests at the side. I read the three characters as numerals forming 239, or perhaps 339, which, referred to the era of A.D. 78, would give either A.D. 317 or 417. The latter is the preferable date, as the period of Kidâra can be fixed with some certainty in the first half of the fifth century A.D. We learn from the Chinese notices that his expedition to the South of the Caucasus was caused by the pressure of the White Huns, before whom he at first retired to the westward, and afterwards crossed the mountains into Kipin or Kophene. The victorous Ephthalites continued their advance to the westward until they reached Merv. There they were encountered by Varahrân V., who defeated them with great slaughter in A.D. 428. Their king Tâtân was killed and his queen captured. Narses, the brother of the Persian king, was appointed Governor of Khorasân, with his residence at Balkh. The retirement of Kitolo before the advance of the White Huns must therefore be placed earlier than A.D. 428—or, say, about A.D. 425, or perhaps even earlier.

The Ephthalites remained quiet during the reign of *Solien Khan*, A.D. 431-443; but on the accession of *Chu-Khan*, the *Konkha* or *Kounkhas* of Priscus, war again broke out, and lasted from A.D. 443 to 456. In the middle of this period the historian Priscus was in the camp of the great Hun conqueror Attila, where he first heard of the Οὔννοι-Κιδαρῖται. These two names I would now separate by identifying the *Huns* with the Ephthalites, and the *Kidaritæ* with the Little Kushâns, whose kingdom was established by Kidâra. The family name of *Kidâra* is found repeated on all the gold and copper coins of the Panjâb which can be assigned to this period, including the later money of Toramâna and his son Pravarasena of Kashmir. The name is also recorded by the early Muhammadan writers as *Kitormân* and *Kitorân*; and it still exists in Kâfiristan, as the chiefs of Chitrâl now proudly style themselves *Shah Kitor*. In A.D. 1030 Alberuni mentions the Kitormân kings. Two centuries later Changiz Khan, after his campaign in the Hindu Kush, wintered in *Buya Kitor*, and nearly two hundred years still later the country of the *Kitor* Kâfirs was invaded by Timur.[1]

Kitolo himself is said to have conquered five different countries or provinces to the north of Gandhâra (or Kandahâr).[2] No names are given; but I conclude that his kingdom included *Ghazni* and *Kâbul* on the west, with *Nagarahâra* and *Chitrâl* in the middle, and *Gandhâra* with *Udyâna* on the east. Kitolo established his son in Gandhâra, with Purushâwar as his capital, and then returned to the west to oppose the Ephthalites. The Chinese record that these Little Kushâns had coins of gold and silver, a fact which is attested by my coins of Kidâra himself as well as of Pravarasena in both metals. One gold coin of Kidâra was extracted by myself from the Stûpa of Baoti Pind, a few miles to the north-west of Shah-dheri or Taxila. Other coins in gold, with the tribal title of Kidâra written perpendicularly under the king's arm, present the names of *Sri Sila*, *Sri Kritavîrya*, *Sri Viswa*, *Sri Kusala*, and *Sri Prakâsa* in the margin. All of these were no doubt the successors of *Kidâra* in the north-west Panjâb (see Figs. 10 to 15, Plate VI.).

Towards the end of the fifth century the Little Kushâns, or *Kidaritæ*, as I think they may be called, were expelled from Gandhâra by an irruption of the Ephthalites or White Huns. The leader of this invasion is called *Laelih* by Sung-yun, and his date is placed at two generations prior to the accession of the king who was reigning in A.D. 520, or say from forty to fifty years before A.D. 515; or in A.D. 465 to 475. The rule of the *Kidaritæ* had, there-

---

[1] *Sir H. Yule*, ii. 584, note.

[2] *Les Huns Blancs*, in passage translated by Julien, p. 43; also Rémusat, *Nouv. Mélanges*, i. 223.

fore, lasted for only forty or fifty years, or from A.D. 425. A Kidarite gold coin was found by Masson in No. 10 Stûpa at Hiddâ, in company with gold coins of Theodosius II., Marcian, and Leo.[3] As the last of these Emperors died in A.D. 474, the Little Kushâns must have been ruling until about that time—what, then, became of the *Kidaritæ* after the Ephthalite conquest? They were certainly expelled from Gandhâra, but they still continued to hold dominion in other districts, as their coins of later dates are very numerous. I conclude therefore that they retired to the north into Chitrâl and Gilgit to the west of the Indus, and to Pakhali and Kashmir to the east of the river.

But the rule of the White Huns on the Upper Indus was brought to a close about A.D. 540 or 545 by the defeat and death of Mihir Kul, the son of *Toramâna.* The White Huns had pushed their conquests into Sindh and Malwa, and even into Gwalior and the valley of the Ganges. But their victorious career in India was checked by the crushing defeat of Mihir Kul at *Kahror*, near Multân.[4] The Hindu Princes, *Nara Sinha Gupta,* of Magadha, and *Yasodharman,* of Mâlwa, combined with others against the common enemy, and after his defeat the *Kidaritæ* of the Upper Indus must have recovered much of their former dominions. There they continued to reign and to strike coins in gold and copper, all stamped with their tribal name of Kidâra. Their rule lasted for three centuries until Kanak, "the last of the Kitormân kings," was sup-

---

[3] *Ariana Antiqua*, Pl. XVIII., 26.

[4] Beal's *Hwen Thsang*, i. 169; Sachau's *Alberuni*, ii. 6; *Vassilief's Târânâth*, by M. La Comme, p. 51, note. *Kahror*, the place where Mihir Kul was defeated, is a large town between Bahâwalpur and Multân.

planted by his Brahman minister about A.D. 850. But even after their tribal name fell into disuse the types of their coinage still lingered on the money of Kashmir for four centuries longer down to the Muhammadan conquest.

Shortly after the death of Mihir Kul, the Jâbuli king of the conquering Huns, the *Kidâras* must have regained possession of *Taxila* or *Shah-dheri*, as I believe that this famous city received the latter name from its being the residence of the *Shâhi* kings. As to the successors of Kidâra they inherited this well-known title of the great Kushân sovereigns. Thoughout the native history of Kashmir these kings are generally styled *Shâhi*, or simply "the Shâhi," and their dominion the *Shâhi-râjya*. Towards the middle of the seventh century the Karkota kings of Kashmir got possession of Taxila and the country of the Salt Range.[5] The Shâhis then retired to the west of the Indus, with Ohind as their capital. But even at so late a date as A.D. 900, the reigning king, *Lalliya Shâhi*, is said to be "amongst kings like the sun amongst the stars."[6]

Al Beruni, who wrote in A.D. 1030, also speaks of the *Shâhiya* kingdom as having existed for about sixty generations or reigns; but he adds that "this *Hindu Shâhiya* dynasty is now extinct." It became extinct by the death of Bhîma Pâla, the son of Trilochana Pâla, in A.D. 1026. He was the last of the family which had so

---

[5] Beal's *Hwen Thsang*.

[6] *Raja Tarangini*, v. 154. Troyer calls him "the illustrious Sâhi, of the country of Lalli." But the original has *Srîmal-Lalliya Sâhi*, which clearly refers to a man and not to a country. *Srî-mân* is a common honorific title of kings. The learned translator also has made a mistake in identifying the *country* of Sâhi with the petty hamlet of *Sâhi-hati*, on the road from Simla to the Satlej. *Hati* means a Baniya's shop. I know the place well.

resolutely opposed the Ghazni kings for upwards of half a century. From this family the rajas of Kashmir took wives on the same terms as they received them from the rajas of Kangra. Shâhi queens are frequently mentioned, and particular mention is made of the Shâhi Vasantalekha, the favourite queen of Harsha, who became a Sati after his death in A.D. 1101.

According to Ferishta the Indian kings who opposed Sabuktagin and his son Mahmud were Brâhmans[7]; and apparently Al Beruni says the same. His words are: "After him (*i.e.*, after Kalar, the Brâhman) ruled the Brâhman kings Sâmand, Kamalu, Bhîm, Jaypâl, Anandpâl, Tarojan-pâl." It is a curious fact that not a single coin has yet been found of any of the Pâl kings, although the money of Jaypâl's predecessors is very common. Both Thomas and Elliot have referred to this change of name as probably indicating a change of family. That there must have been a change of family seems to me to be absolutely certain, for the simple reason that no Brahman can be named Pâl. The change in the ruling family is further proved by Ferishta's statement that Jaypâl was the son of Ishtpâl, or Aṣatpâl, and not of his predecessor Bhîma, or Bhîma Deva, as he is named on his coins. That Trilochan Pâl was not a Brâhman is shown by his proposal to wed his son Bhîm Pâl to the daughter of the great Rajput Raja Chandra Rai.

Masudi, who wrote not later than A.D. 950, and therefore before the accession of Jaypâl, states that the King of Kandahâr [Gandhâra] is called *Ḥahaj*, and that "this name is common to all the kings of that country."[8] He

---

[7] Briggs, i. 15, and Sachau's *Al Beruni*, ii. 13.
[8] Elliot's *Historians*, i. 22.

adds that "Kandahâr is the country of the Rajput," the family name cannot refer to the Brâhman predecessors of *Jaipâl*, but rather to *Aṣat-pâl*, his father and his ancestors. I prefer to read the family name as *Jajaha*, and to identify it with that of the *Janjuha* Rajputs, who have formed a large part of the population of the Salt Range for many centuries. Baber writes the name as *Janjuha*, which is still in use; but the commoner form at the present day is *Januha*. Abul Fazl also uses this form, and states that the warlike Mewâtis, who are all Muhammadans, were converted *Januhas*.[9] The Maâsir writes the name as جانوهه *Jânuha*. I would therefore identify these *Janjuhas* with the *Jajaha* of Masudi.

I have already mentioned the gold coins bearing the names of *Sri Sila* [- -], *Sri Kritavîrya*, *Sri Viswa*, *Sri Kusala*, and *Sri Prakâṣa*, all of whom I take to have been the successors of *Kitolo*, as they give his name under the king's arm in the Indian form of *Kidâra*. As none of these names is found in the Kashmir list, I conclude that the kings themselves must have reigned in the country to the west of Kashmir—in Shah-dheri and Mansera to the east of the Indus, and in Yasin and Chitrâl to the west of that river. In fact, a coin of *Sri Sila* [- -] was found in No. 10 Tope at Hidda, in company with coins of Theodosius, Marcian, and Leo, who reigned from A.D. 450 to 474.[10]

But there are other coins with the name of *Kidâra* which undoubtedly belong to Kashmir. The earliest are the well-known copper pieces of *Toramâna*, and the gold and silver coins of his son *Pravarasena*. The former coins

---

[9] Blochmann's *Ain Akbari*, i. 456 and 377.
[10] *Ariana Antiqua*, Pl. XVIII., 26.

are actually mentioned in the Raja Tarangini [iii. 103] under the name of *Bâlahat.* The story is that Toramâna, the younger brother of Raja Hiranya, "ayant supprimé la multitude des petites monnaies qui avaient cours, répandit des dinares frappés en son propre nom."[11] The king resented this disrespect, and cast his brother into prison, where he died. It is this prisoner, *who never reigned* at all, that Bhau Dâji and Râjendra Lâl have strangely attempted to identify with *Toramâna Jaüvla,* the father of Mihir Kul and the conqueror of Sindh and Mâlwa.

The native translator of the Raja Tarangini[12] differs slightly from Troyer in his rendering of the passage about the coins struck by Toramâna. He says that the young prince "forbade the use of the coins struck by King *Vâla,* and largely circulated the *Dînnaras* coined by himself." The expression in the original is *Bâlâhatânâm,* which means simply the "money of Bâla." But *hăt* in Kashmir is also the actual name of one particular coin, which was so called because it was of the value of "one hundred" *ganis.* This is clearly proved by Abul Fazl's account of the coins of Kashmir. The list is as follows:—[13]

2 Bârah-ganis [or *twelvers*]	=	1 Panchi [or *twenty-fiver*]
4 Panchis . . .	=	1 Hăt [or *hundreder*]
10 Hăts . . .	=	1 Sâsnu [or *thousander*]
100 Sâsnus . . .	=	1 Lakh [or 1,00,000]

Bârah for twelve is as old as Asoka's inscriptions:—*Hăt* is the western form of *Săt*=100; and *Sâs* is the common contraction for *Sahasra*=1,000, as in *Sâs-bahu* for *Sahasra-bahu,* the thousand armed Arjuna. But there is a still more striking proof of the value of *hăt,* as its initial

---

[11] Troyer's translation.
[12] Jogesh Chunder Dutt. Calcutta, 1879.
[13] Gladwin's *Ain Akbari,* ii. 126.

letter ϩ of the Gandharian alphabet is used in all the Indo-Scythian and Gupta inscriptions as the symbol for 100.

As the existing coins of Toramâna, which are found in considerable numbers in Kashmir, are confined to one class of copper pieces, ranging from 100 to 120 grains in weight, it seems not improbable that what Toramâna did was to collect the old coins called *Bâla-hăts*, and to recoin them as *Dinârs* in his own name. According to Abul Fazl the *hăt* of Kashmir was equal to the *dâm* of Akbar, or $\frac{1}{40}$th of a rupee. But the *dâm* weighs 320 grains, whereas the *hăts* of Toramâna do not exceed 120 grains. The money thus recoined I take to have been the barbarous pieces of the later Kushân princes, whose names are unknown.[14] These pieces vary in weight from 100 to 125 grains, with the king standing on the obverse, and Siva and his Bull on the reverse. The coins of Toramâna and his son Pravarasena are so superior in execution to these coïns and to all the contemporary coins of North-west India, that I look upon them as the first real issue of the Kashmir mint. There was no previous king of Kashmir named Bâla, and I much doubt whether there was any previous coinage in Kashmir. In fact Kashmir was or had been generally a tributary province. It was certainly tributary to Asoka Maurya, to the Kushân King Kanishka, and to the White Hun Mihir Kul.

I suppose that the title of *Bâla* refers to the "great king" of the Kushâns, who had been the suzerain of Kashmir, and that the money called *Bâla-hăt* was so named after the "great king"—the *Bâla-Rao* of those

---

[14] See Thomas, *Prinsep's Antiquities*, Pl. VIII. Figs. 6 and 7, for two specimens of these coins.

times. The coins themselves are very rude copies of the money of the Kushân king Vâsu Deva, the last prince whose name can be traced on the coins. The Greek characters become more and more corrupt. The letter **B** generally remains distinct, but the name reads like **BIΛO** or **BIΓO**. It is just possible that the name of Raja Bâla may have been derived from these rude coins. One coin, in fact, actually has **BOΛO**. All the copper Kushân coins of Mathura and Sankisa have **BIΛO** or **BIΓO**. I incline, therefore, rather to doubt the existence of any early Kushân king named *Bâla*, and to accept the derivation of the name from *Bâla*, the "great or superior." There is another class of small copper coins of the later Kushân period, which may perhaps be the *Bâlà-hăt* mintage referred to. They have on the obverse Siva and his Bull (very rude), and on the reverse a symbol which I take to be a rude fire-altar, and on the right the name of *Bâla* in monograms of Indian letters. But whatever may have been the origin of the name, I consider that the money of Toramâna and his son Pravarasena was the initial coinage of the Kashmir mint.

The effort which produced these coins seems to have relaxed rather suddenly, as I cannot refer to any specimen of the subsequent coinage of Kashmir, which can be placed earlier than the accession of Durlabha Vardhana, the first raja of the Nâga dynasty.

Whether my identification of the reigning family of Gandhâra in the tenth century with the last of the Kushân princes be correct or not, I still adhere to my opinion that *Jaipâl* and his successors were Rajputs and not Brâhmans. I have already noted the fact that *Trilochan-pâl* had proposed to wed his son *Bhîmpâl* to the daughter of the great Rajput Chandor Rai, Raja of Sirwâwa, "one of the greatest men in Hind," as Utbi calls him.[15] This fact alone is sufficient to show that the family could not have been Brâhmans.

Albiruni distinctly makes Trilochanpâl a descendant of the Tûrk king Kanishka who built the monastery at Purushâwar. He calls the dynasty the "Shâhiya of Kâbul," and says that the descendants ruled for about sixty generations. Writing in A.D. 1030, after the death of Trilochanpâl, he says, "this *Shâhiya* dynasty is now extinct."[16] The author of the Raja Tarangini says the same thing, that by the death of Trilochanpâl the Shâhi dynasty came to an end.[17] The round number of sixty descendants counted as reigns shows that Albiruni looked upon this Shâhi dynasty as the actual descendants of the great Kushân king Kanishka. Taking the mean length of a reign at fifteen years, the actual Indian average, the date of Trilochanpâl will fall nine hundred years after Kanishka, or after A.D. 100 = A.D. 1000, in the reign of Mahmûd of Ghazni, the conqueror of the Shâhi kings.

The result of this discussion shows that *Jaipâl*, the successor of the four Brâhman kings, was not himself a Brâhman, and was almost certainly a Kushân chief who was accepted as a Rajput. I conclude that on the weakening of the Brâhman rule at Kâbul by the attacks of the Muhammadans under Yâkub and Amru bin Lais, A.D. 873—900, the predecessors of Jaipâl had gradually recovered the former influence of the family. Jaipâl is the first of these Rajputs who is recorded to have fought with Sabuktigin. The two armies met near Langhân in A.H. 372, or

[15] Târikh-i-Yamîmi in Elliot's *Muhammadan Historians*, ii. 147.

[16] Sachau's *Albiruni*, ii. pp. 10, 11, 13.

[17] *Raja Tarangini*, B. vii, slok, 66.

A.D. 982. In a second great battle fought with Mahmûd in A.H. 392, or A.D. 1001, near Purushâwar, the Hindus were defeated, and lost nearly all of their territory to the west of the Indus, retaining only *Wehand.* Jaipâl was then an old man, and, seeing that he was a "captive in the prison of old age and degradation," he put an end to himself by burning.[18] That he was then a very old man is proved by the fact that his *grandsons* and *sons* were taken prisoners along with himself; and one of these *grandsons,* Brâhman-Pâl, the son of Anand-Pâl, only a few years later opposed Mahmûd near Wehand "at the head of a valiant army," when "the battle lasted from morning till evening, and the infidels were near gaining the victory." The accession of Jaipâl cannot, therefore, be placed later than A.D. 960, and that of his father, Aṣatpâl in A.D. 930. As the Brâhman Kamlüa was reigning in A.D. 900, and was succeeded by his son Bhima Deva, the latter must have been contemporary with Aṣat-pâl. To this Aṣat-pâl, the father of Jaipâl, I would ascribe the ascendancy of the Rajput family, and the consequent fall of the Brâhman dynasty.

---

18 "Utbi," in Elliot's *Muhammadan Historians.*

The succession of these two families I make out to be as follows :—

Brâhmans.		
	Albiruni.	Coins.
840	Kalar . . .	SPALAPATI .
860	Sâmand . . .	SAMANTA-DEVA
900	Kamlu (Kamlad ?) .	KHAMARADAK .
920	Bhima . . .	BHIMA-DEVA .

Kushâns.		
825	Kanak . . .	VENKA.
		Rajputs.
875	— —	Lalliya Shâhi.
900	— —	Toramâna Shâhi.
925	AṢAT-PAL . .	?
950	JAI-PAL . .	Jaya Pâla Shâhi.
1002	ANAND-PAL .	Ananda-Pâla Shâhi.
1012	TRILOCHAN-PAL	Trilochana Pâla.
1021	BHIM-PAL . .	Bhima-Pâla Shâhi.
1026	End of Dynasty.	

The Shâhi kings, the antagonists of the Ghazni Sultans, were the descendants of the Little Kushâns or Kidaritæ. But what has become of the mass of the Kushâns of the Kâbul Valley? In my opinion, they are now represented by the *Kâfirs* of Chitrâl, who still hold the southern slopes of the Indian Caucasus to the north of the Kâbul River. On the occupation of the Kâbul Valley by the White Huns the Kushâns would naturally have retired to the hills, where they still preserve much of their ancient religion, customs, and language, together with their tribal name of *Koresh* or *Goresh*.[19] In these names I recognise the **KORSAN** of the coins and the *Kushân* and *Gushân* of the inscriptions. Their claim to a descent from Alexander points to the same conclusion, that they are the descendants of the immediate successors of the Greeks. It is quite possible that some portions of the tribe may have found refuge in the hills to the south of the Kâbul Valley, where the old name would seem to be preserved in the *Koreshan* of Dera Ismail Khan, and the *Goreshan* of Dera Ghâzi Khan.

As the chief of Chitrâl still bears the title of "Shah Kitor," I presume that the name of *Kitor* gradually prevailed over the old name of *Kushân*, and that *all* the *Kâfirs* of the present day are simply *unconverted* Kushâns. Mahmûd of Ghazni kept a large body of mercenary troops, who were commanded by Tilak of Hind. He (Tilak) afterwards brought many *Hindu Kitors* under the rule of Masâud.[20] Two centuries later Changiz Khan, after his campaign in the Hindu Kush, wintered in the mountains of *Buya Kitor*. Nearly two hundred years later, in A.D.

---

[19] Dr. Bellew's *Ethnography of Afghanistan*, pp. 143, 144.
[20] Elliot's *Muhammadan Historians of India*, ii. 127.

1398, Timur describes the people as of "powerful form and of fair complexion," and adds that "their language was distinct from Turki, Persian, Hindi, and Kashmiri."[21] They had a local era of their own which Timur added to the Hijra date of 800 in his rock inscription describing his victory over them.

---

[21] Elliot's *Muhammadan Historians of India*, iii. 401.

DESCRIPTION OF THE PLATE.

No.	Metal.	Inches.	Grains.		Plate.
				KIDÂRA SHÂHI. [Author.]	
1	Æ	1·10	56	*Bust of the King* to the front, with bushy hair on both sides of the face, like the Sassanian Kings; crown with triple ornament; long earrings. Indian inscription in early Gupta letters, *Kidâra Kushâna Shâhi*, the last letter, *hi*, being close to the face on the right. *Rev.*—*Fire-altar*, with two attendants carrying drawn swords, or perhaps the *Barsom*. Below the altar are three characters, which I take for numerals. They are the same on all my three specimens, although the coins are from different dies. I read them as 339, which, if referred to the Saka era, would be 339 + 78 = A.D. 417.	VI. 1
2	Æ	1·10	56	[Duplicate, of similar types.]	VI. 2
				[Author.]	
3	AV	0·85	118	King standing to left, as on the earlier Kushân coins of Kanishka and his successors. Indian letters or monograms in three places. To right, *Kushâna*; under King's arm, *Kidâra*; to left, *Kapan* (? for *Kophane*). I conclude, "The Kushân King KIDARA of Kapan." *Rev.*—The goddess *Ardokhsho* (Lakshmi), seated on throne,	VI. 3

				with cornucopiæ in her left hand. I found a duplicate of this coin in the Baoti-pind Stûpa, to the north of Hadon Abdal. [Author.]	
4	AV	0·85	121	King standing as on No. 3. To the left, in Indian letters, perpendicularly arranged, *Sri Shâhi;* and to the right, under the King's arm, *Kidâra*. *Rev.*—Goddess, seated, holding trident in left hand. Indian inscription on right, *Kidâra*, in rather later characters. [Author.]	VI. 4
5	Æ	1·10	56	Bust of the King to the front, with bushy hair on both sides of the face, and triple ornament on head-dress, like that on *Kidâra's* silver coins. Long streamers rise up from the shoulders, as on the Sassanian coins. *Rev.*—Fire-altar, with attendant, on left. Uncertain object on right. [Author.]	VI. 5
6	Æ	1·0	53	Bust of King to the front, resting on a large crescent; bushy side hair, like that of the Sassanian Kings. Crown similar to that worn by Sapor III., surmounted by crescent and ball. Two letters, like Indian, to right (? = *Bhasa*). *Rev.*—Not distinguishable.	VI. 6

DESCRIPTION OF THE PLATE—*continued.*

No.	Metal.	Inches.	Grains.		Plate.
				[Author.]	
7	Æ	1·10	54	Bust of King, full-face, with bushy side hair. Lappets flying from shoulders. *Rev.*—Not distinguishable.	VI. 7
				[Author. From the Bannu Valley.]	
8	Æ	0·55	31	Male bust, full-face, surrounded by a circle of beads. *Rev.*—Inscription, in two lines, of Indian letters of Indo-Scythian period, *Kshatrapa Tarîka.*	VI. 8
				[Author. From the Bannu Valley.]	
9	Æ	0·55	31	Male bust to left, surrounded by a circle of beads. *Rev.*—Inscription, in two lines, as on No. 8, *Kshatrapa Tarîka.*	VI. 9
				[Brit. Museum. Author.]	
10	AV	0·75	120	King standing to the left, as on No. 3. Under the King's arm, *Kidâra*, in Indian letters. To the left, below the King's hand, *Iṣa*, in Indian letters. *Rev.*—Seated goddess, as on No. 3. To right, *Sri Visva*, in Indian letters.	VI. 10
				[Author.]	
11	AV	0·75	120	King standing to left, as on No. 3. Under King's arm,	VI. 11

				Kidâra, in Indian letters. To left, under King's hand, *Dharva*. *Rev.*—Seated goddess, as on No. 3. To right, *Sri Kṛitavîrya*, in Indian letters. [Author.]	
12	AV,	0·75	119	King standing to left, as No. 3; under his arm, *Kidâra;* to left, ——*vaṁ*. *Rev.*—Seated goddess. To right, *Sri Siladitya*, in Indian letters. [Author.]	VI. 12
13	AV	0·80	113	King standing to left, as on No. 3. *Kidâra* under the arm, in Indian letters. To the left, below, *dhavaṁ* (?); the first letter is uncertain. *Rev.*—Goddess, seated. To right, *Sri Kusala*, in Indian letters. [Pale gold. Author. From Gandgarh Hill.]	VI. 13
14	AV,	0·95	116	King standing to left, as on No. 3. To left, *Sri Shâhi;* and under the arm, *Kidâra*, both in Indian letters. *Rev.*—Goddess, seated. Uncertain letter on right. [Pale gold. Author. From Gandgarh Hill.]	VI. 14
15	AV,	0·95	118	King standing to left, as on No. 3. Under his arm, *Kidâra;* and to the right, *Sri Prakâṣa*, both in Indian letters. *Rev.*—Goddess, seated, as on the last.	VI. 15

LATER INDO-SCYTHIANS.

EPHTHALITES, OR WHITE HUNS.

BY

MAJOR-GENERAL SIR A. CUNNINGHAM, R.E.,
K.C.I.E., C.S.I.

REPRINTED FROM THE NUMISMATIC CHRONICLE,
VOL. XIV., THIRD SERIES, PAGES 243—293.

LONDON:
1894.

LATER INDO-SCYTHIANS.[1]

EPHTHALITES, OR WHITE HUNS.

(See Plates IX.—XII.)

THE earliest notice that we possess of the great horde of Ephthalites or White Huns, who took Khorasan from the Sassanians and overran Northern India, is by the historian Priscus. It was in the camp of Attila, in A.D. 448, that he first heard of the Οὔννοι Κιδαρῖται. The next notice is by Kosmas Indikopleustes, who in A.D. 530 mentions *Gollas*, king of the Λευκοὶ Οὔννοι, on the west bank of the Indus. He calls their country Οὐννία, again giving the name without the aspirate. Procopius also, who died in 565, calls them Οὔννους Λευκούς and Ἐφθαλίτας. Theophanes, too, calls them *White Uns* and *Nephthalites*. The aspirate, however, is given by the Armenian writers Elisha and Lazarus, who speak of the *Hunk* and *Kushank*, or *Huns* and *Kushâns*. They are described by the Chinese pilgrim Sung-yun in A.D. 520 under the name of *Yetha*, which is only a shortened form of *Ye-tha-i-li-to*, the original of the Greek Ἐφθαλῖται and of the Muhummadan *Haiathelah* of Firdausi and later

---

[1] This paper was read at the Oriental Congress of 1892 and a portion of it has appeared without illustrations or descriptions in the Transactions of the Congress.

writers. As Sung-yun's description of the *Yetha* tallies exactly with Hwen Thsang's account of the *Himatala* in A.D. 640, we see that this is also a variant form of *Ephthala*. By the Indians they are always called *Hûṇa* or *Hâra Hûṇa*. It seems probable that their Chinese name of *Yuan-Yuan* may have been the original of the Indian *Hûṇa*.

The earliest Indian notice of the *Húṇas* is in the Bhitari inscription of Skanda Gupta, A.D. 450 to 480, where the king is said to have "joined in close conflict with the *Húṇas*."[2] According to the pilgrim Sung-yun, who was in Gandhâra in A.D. 520, two generations had already passed away since the Hûṇa conquest, when the Yethas set up *Lae-lih* as king.[3] As the accession of Mihirkul, who was then reigning, is now generally accepted as about A.D. 515, the conquest of Gandhâra and the enthronement of *Lae-lih* must be placed about fifty years earlier, or in A.D. 465 to 470, or towards the end of Skanda Gupta's reign. As Skanda Gupta possessed Mâlwa and Gujarât, the *Húṇas* probably came into conflict with the Indians on the Lower Indus.

According to the Chinese writers, the White Huns first appeared in the countries on the Oxus in the beginning of the fifth century, when *Shelun*, the son of the *Tsanyu* (or *Shanyu*) of the *Jwan-jwan* (or *Yuan-Yuan*), retired to the west with his brother. After defeating *Payekhi*, the king of the *Hiungnu*, he gave up the title of *Tsanyu* and assumed that of *Kieu-teu-fa Khâkân*. In 410 A.D. he was defeated by the Wei Tartars, and died during his flight. His brother *Hulu* succeeded him, and was followed in 414 by his nephew *Puluchin*, who was killed by his cousin

---

[2] Fleet's *Inscriptions of the Guptas*, p. 56.
[3] Beal's *Chinese Pilgrims*, i. 100.

Tâtân in 425. The new king began his reign by the invasion of the north-east provinces of Persia; but, being vigorously attacked by the Sassanian king *Varahran V.*, he was defeated and killed near Merv in 428 A.D. His whole camp, with his queen, the *Khâtun*, and his rich crown set with gems, all fell into the hands of the conqueror.

Tâtân was succeeded by his son *Uti*, who took the title of *Solien Khan*. He would appear to have been the real founder of the Ephthalite power, as he received a Chinese princess in marriage and gave his own sister to the Emperor of China. He carried on a nine years' war with Isdegerd II. of Persia, from 443 to 451 A.D., and eventually, about 456, forced him to retire to his own dominions to the south of the Oxus. From this time the empire of the White Huns became very powerful until 554, when *Solien-teu-fa Khan* was defeated by *Tumen*, the "Grand Shahu" of the Turks. During this century of their prosperity the dominion of the White Huns was extended on all sides, until, as described by Sung-yun in 520, it embraced all the countries lying between *Persia* on the west and *Khotan* on the east to *Tieh-li* on the south. *Tieh-li* I would identify with *Dahal* or the kingdom of *Chedi* on the Narbada, over which Mihirkul must have held sway in succession to his father *Toramâṇa*. During this century about a dozen different kings ruled over the Ephthalites on the Oxus. I now give their names on Chinese authority,[4] as I think it probable that hereafter we may be able to assign to them some of our numerous unread coins.

---

[4] D'Herbelot, *Bibliothèque Orientale*.

A.D.	Name.	Title.	Remarks.
402	SHELUN	*Kieu-teu-fa-Khâkân*	..
410	Hu-lu	Brother of Shelun	..
414	Pu-lu-chin	Nephew of Shelun	Killed by *Tâtân*.
425	TÂ-TÂN	Cousin of Shelun	Killed in battle with Varahran V., 428
428	U-TI	*Solien Khan*	..
443	Tu-ho-chin	*Chu-Khan*	Κούγχας of Priscus; war with Isdegerd II.
464	YU-CHIN	*Shulo-Puchin Khan*	*Khush Nawâz* of Firdausi; war with Feroz.
485	Teu-lun	*Fu-ku-shun*	*Faganish* of Firdausi; restored Kobad.
492 } 494 }	..	*Apotilo;* revolts	Retires to west with 100,000 followers.
..	No-kai, joint emperor	*Heu-khi-fu-tai*	..
..	Futu	*Ta-khan-Khan*	..
508	Cheu-neu	*Tu-lo fu-pe-teu-fa*	..
520	Shifa	Rebels	..
521	*O-no-wei*	*So-lien-teu-piu-teu-fa*	..
..	*Po-lo-men*	Joint ruler	..
534	*O-no-wei*	Sole Khakan	Defeated by Turks in 546.
546	*Ghan-lo-chin*	..	Defeated by Turks in 554.
554	..	MUHAN-KHAN	of the TURKS.

The connection of the White Huns with India cannot be traced till near the end of the fifth century, from which time they may be looked upon as a separate branch of the Indo-Scythian conquerors, or the "Indian Ephthalites." Their history, as far as I have been able to trace it, begins with Lae-lih, the father of *Toramâṇa* and grandfather of *Mihirakula* or *Mihirgul*. Both the last kings were rulers of the Panjâb, and both made conquests in India in the early part of the sixth century A.D., while the main horde remained in possession of the countries to the north of the Indian Caucasus, with Gorgo as their capital (Procopius, A.D. 540). The following points in their history are derived from six different authorities:—

I. *Sung-yun*, Chinese pilgrim, A.D. 520.

In A.D. 520 Sung-yun entered Gandhâra, where he found that the reigning king was an Ephthalite (*Ye-tha-i-li-to*) who *did not believe in Buddha.* He was warlike, and kept 700 war-elephants.[5] Peshawur was on his frontier, and he had been at war with Kipin for three years regarding his boundary. The pilgrim adds that "*it was formerly called the country of Yepolo,*" and that since the conquest by the Yethas, who set up *Lae-lih* to be king, two generations had passed away.

II. *Kosmas Indikopleustes*, A.D. 522—530.

"In India further up the country, *i.e.*, further north, are the White Huns. The king, named *Gollas*, 'tis said, goes forth to war with not less than 1,000 elephants, besides a great force of cavalry. *This ruler tyrannizes over India.* Once when he laid siege to a certain inland city of India, protected all round by water . . . his army drank up all the water, and he took the city."

III. *Hwen Tshang*, Chinese pilgrim, A.D. 630.

In the old town of She-kie-lo [Ṣâkala or Sangala] formerly reigned King *Mihirakula*. *He ruled over India*, and conquered the neighbouring provinces. Bâlâditya king of Magadha, having refused to pay tribute, Mihirakula invaded his kingdom. *Bâlâditya retired to a morass.* The invader was taken prisoner, and afterwards released. As his brother had established himself in Ṣâkala, Mihirakula went to Kashmir, where he killed the king,

---

[5] Beal, vol. i. p. xcix.

and afterwards did the same in Gandhâra. He persecuted Buddhists, overthrew stûpas, and demolished monasteries.

IV. *Târanâth,* History of Buddhism in India.

In the time of *Dharmachandra,* king of Magadha, a Turushka ruled in Kashmir, and *Hunimanta,* king of Persia, ruled over Lahore and Multan. One day, seeing on his queen's dress the footprint mark of the king of Magadha, he was affronted, and invaded the country of Magadha, where he demolished the temples of Buddha. Then Buddhapaksha, Raja of Benares, with the aid of other princes of West and South India, attacked Hunimanta, and killed him, and *re-established the religion of Buddha.*

V. *Raja Tarangini,* History of Kashmir.

I. 289.—Mihirakula, son of Mukula, on seeing the golden footprint of the king of Ceylon on his wife's dress, invaded Ceylon and killed the king. He was as cruel as death (*Yama*). He persecuted Buddhists, and built a temple to the sun as *Mihireswara.*

VI. *Chach-Nâma,* History of Sindh.

After the capture of Multân by Muhammad Kâsim in A.D. 173, he was informed that "in ancient times there was a chief in this city whose name was *Jibawin* [or *Jabüin,* جبوين], and who was a descendant of the Rai of Kashmir. . . . He made a reservoir on the eastern side of Multân. In the middle of it he built a temple . . . (which contained) an idol made of red gold." This was the famous temple of the sun-god, which was a great object of worship for many centuries. The popularity of the sun-god of Multân is vouched for by Al Beruni (Sachau, ii. 148, 184). The Sâhis are said to have reigned for 137 years.

Inscription of TORAMÂṆA *from Kyura, Panjâb.*

In this inscription from the Salt Range in the North-West Punjâb the king is called *Mahârâja* TORAMÂṆA *Shâha* JAÜVLA. The title of *Jaüvla* occurs twice. I notice this because on my silver coins it is spelt *Jabubla* or *Jabuvla*. The date of this inscription is unfortunately too much injured to be readable.

Inscription of TORAMÂṆA *from Eran in Mâlwa.*

The inscription is dated in the *first* year of Mahârâjâdhirâja TORAMÂṆA.

Inscription of MIHIRAKULA *from Gwalior Fort.*

This inscription was found by myself in 1844, built into the wall of the fort of Gwalior, near the Suraj-kund. Mr. Fleet describes it as a record of the building of a temple of the sun in the fifteenth year of the reign of MIHIRAKULA, the lord of the earth, the son of TORAMÂNA.

Inscriptions of YASÓDHARMAN *from Mandasor in Mâlwa.*

In these inscriptions it is recorded that *Yasodharman* possessed countries which "not even the *Guptas* and *Hûṇas* could subdue . . . and that homage was done to him by even the famous King MIHIRAKULA." One o the inscriptions is dated in the *Mâlava* year 589, or A.D. 532.

Jyotirvidâbharana, xxii. 17.

"In a great battle he [Vikrama of Ujain] conquered the king of *Ṣakas* in *Ruma*, paraded his royal prisoner in Ujjayini, and afterwards set him free." As this Vikrama of Mâlwa is said to be the contemporary of Varâha Mihira and the "Nine Gems," we learn that his date was the first half of the sixth century A.D.

Raja Tarangini, iii. 125—128, 330.

125. "At the same time [when Pravarasena was young] Srîmân Vikramâditya, also named Harsha, ruled in Ujjayini as Emperor of all India."

128. "Having first destroyed the Sakas," &c.

330. "He [Pravarasena] restored to his father's throne the son of Vikramâditya of (Mâlava), who was named Pratâpaṣîla by some, and Sîlâditya by others."

Hwen Thsang, Chinese Pilgrim, 629—642 A.D.

"Sixty years ago flourished *Sílâditya* [King of Mâlava]." As the pilgrim visited Mâlwa in A.D. 640, Sîlâditya's date must be 580 A.D., and his father Vikramâditya's date the first half of the sixth century. The pilgrim also visited Sindh in A.D. 641,[6] when the king was a *Shu-to-lo* or Sudra. But as we know from Sungyun and Kosmas that the White Huns were then ruling on the Indus, I would suggest that the first syllable, *shu*,

---

[6] See *Ancient Geography of India*, p. 566, for this date.

may be a mistake for *fa*, as these two characters are so much alike that they are frequently mistaken. This change would make the name *Fa-tu-lo*, which might be accepted for Ephthala. It is, however, quite possible that the pilgrim may have looked upon a White Hun as a Sudra.

Albiruni, A.D. 1030.

In his account of the Vikrama and Ṣaka eras, Albiruni gives his opinion that the Vikramâditya, from whom the era got its name, was not identical with that one who killed the Ṣaka king, but only a namesake. I came to the same conclusion myself when I found at Gyârispur the first inscription dated in the "Era of the Mâlavas" (936 of the Mâlava Kâla), which I at once presumed to be the same as the famous Vikramâditya era (*Archæol. Survey*, x. 34, and Plate XI.). At the same time I hazarded the conjecture, which I communicated to Mr. Fergusson, that the name of Vikramâditya must have been given to the era by the later king of that name, the patron of the "Nine Gems," who reigned in the first half of the sixth century A.D. But Mr. Fergusson went beyond my conjecture, and attributed the original foundation of the era to that king.

TORAMAṆA.

From a comparison of all these authorities I gather the following facts regarding TORAMÂNA and his son MIHIRAKULA.

The leader of the Hûṇas, who established himself on the Indus towards the end of the fifth century A.D., was *Lae-lih*, to whom I would assign the silver coin with the title of *Udayaditya*. His son was TORAMÂṆA, called also Shâha *Jaüvla*, or *Jabuvla*, or *Jabula*. He was the *Jabula*, reading جبول for جبون, or the first of the Shâhis, who built the Temple of the Sun in Multân in A.D. 505. This date is established by deducting the duration of the Shâhi rule in Sindh, 137 years, from A.D. 642, when Chach Brahman rebelled and became king of Sindh. In September, 641, when Hwen Thsang was in Sindh, the king was a *Shu-to-lo*, or, as I have suggested, a *Fatulo* or *Ephthalite*, or perhaps the Chinese pilgrim looked upon him as a Sudra.

Some time later, or about 510 A.D., Toramâṇa had extended his rule to Mâlwa. We know certainly that Budha Gupta was still reigning in 165 and 174 of the Gupta era. The former date is on the Eran pillar, and the latter is the date on one of my silver coins. They correspond with 483 and 492 A.D. The inscription of Bhânu Gupta is dated in A. Gupt. 191, or A.D. 509. The colossal boar at Eran was set up in the first year of Toramâṇa, some time after Budha Gupta.

The small silver coins of Toramâṇa of the Gupta type are dated in 52 of some unknown era. The only *era* that seems possible is that of *Saka*, which a Scythian might be supposed likely to adopt. By adding the omitted hundreds to make 452 Ṣaka, we get 530 A.D., which is a possible date, although I should have preferred an earlier one. The only remarkable date in the history of the White Huns which I can suggest is the final expulsion of the Sassanians from the countries to the north of the Oxus by Chu-khan in A.D. 456 or 457. If the year 52 be reckoned from this point, we get A.D. 508 or 509 for the establishment of Toramâṇa's rule in Mâlwa.

Toramâṇa's preference for solar worship is shown by

his building a temple to the sun in Multân, and by naming his son *Mihir-kul.*

The silver coins of *Toramâṇa* are of two distinct classes —(1.) Broad thin pieces of Sassanian type, bearing the king's head on the obverse, with a club in front of the face. The legend is in Indian letters of Gupta type, *Shâhi Jabublah,* and also *Jabula* on others. *Reverse,* traces of fire-altar and attendants. (2.) Small silver hemidrachms, like those of the Guptas, with the king's head on the obverse, and a peacock with expanded tail on the reverse. The king's face is turned in the opposite direction to that of every one of his Gupta predecessors.[7] In front of the face is the date of 52, which I have previously noticed.

The small copper coins attributed to Toramâṇa are found both in the Panjâb and in the country between the Satlej and Jumna. Their attribution is based on the type of the sun with the abbreviated name of *Tora* in large letters. The same sun-type is found on the copper coins of *Mihirakula,* of which a few specimens show the bull struck over the sun emblem.

---

[7] Mr. Thomas has drawn attention to this change in the direction of the face, which he considered to be *intentional* (*Dynasty of the Guptas,* p. 51, note). I have also noted it as denoting the change of dynasty. But Mr. Vincent Smith thinks that the change is a mere accident, because on the gold coins the horsemen face the right as well as the left. He has overlooked the fact that *every* single silver coin of the Guptas has the face in the same direction. He has also overlooked the fact that the silver coins were the produce of the Mâlwa mints, while the gold coins were the produce of the Gangetic mints. I would suggest also that where the archers and riders hold the bow or the bridle in the *right* hand, the change must have been due to the carelessness of the die-sinker, and not the ambidextrousness of the kings.

As Toramâṇa was the successor of Budha Gupta in Mâlwa, and also the father of Mihirakula, the contemporary of Bâlâditya (Narasinha Gupta), his date must certainly fall about the end of the fifth and the beginning of the sixth century, or from 490 to 515 A.D., allowing perhaps a few years either way.

MIHIRGUL OR MIHIRAKULA.

The career of *Mihirgul* or *Mihirakula* may be briefly sketched from a comparison of the different authorities which I have previously quoted.

Hwen Thsang.—He was the Raja of *Sâkala*, in the Panjâb. Having attacked Bâlâditya, king of Magadha, he was taken prisoner, but was afterwards released. On returning to Sâkala, he found his brother on the throne. He then went to Kashmir, of which he became king by treachery, and afterwards occupied Gandhâra.

Târanâth.—*Hunimanta*, the foreign king of Lahore and Multân, invaded Dharmachandra of Magadha, but was defeated and killed by the combined troops of Central and Southern India. I take *Hunimanta* to be the leader of the *Hûṇas*, and I would identify Dharmachandra with Raja *Yasodharman* of Mâlwa, who records that Mihirakula had paid him homage before A.D. 532.[8]

Raja Tarangini.—*Mihirakula* is recorded as having succeeded his father on the throne of Kashmir, and the invasion of Mlecchas during his father's reign probably refers to the *Hûṇas*. He is also recorded as being a persecutor of Buddhists and a worshipper of the sun, to whom he

[8] See inscription from *Mandisor*.

dedicated the temple of *Mihireswara.* During the reign of his father Kashmir was invaded by *Mlecchas.* His father is variously named as *Mukula* or *Vâsukula* or *Vâmakula.*

Kosmas Indikopleustes, who travelled in A.D. 522—530, names the king of the White Huns *Gollas,* whom I would identify with *Mihir-gul.*

In all these different authors I find the record of a great foreign conqueror in the end of the fifth and beginning of the sixth century A.D., who ruled over the Panjâb, and invaded Northern India, where he reigned for upwards of fifteen years, as the Gwalior inscription of his minister from the temple of the sun is dated in the fifteenth year of his reign.

As I have already identified his father, *Toramâṇa,* with *Jabuna* or *Jabula,* the first Scythian king of Sindh, who built the temple of the sun at Multân, so I would now identify his son Mihirkul with Jabula's successor, who in the Chach-Nâma is called *Sihiras.* As the original Chach-Nâma must have been written in Indian characters, in which the letters *s* and *m* are so much alike as to be frequently interchanged, I think it very probable that the name of this second Scythian king of Sindh was really *Mihira,* and that he was the *Mihir-kul* of our coins and inscriptions.

All the accounts of Mihir-kul agree in the main points of his career :—

1. He was a foreigner, a Mleccha or Hûṇa.

2. He invaded Northern India, at first with success, as we learn by his inscription from Gwalior ; but latterly, after at least fifteen years, he was defeated and obliged to retire.

3. He persecuted Buddhists and patronised Brahmans

and their gods, as we see by the bull of *Siva* and the *Vrisha-dhwaja*, or "bull-ensign," on his coins.

4. His rule generally covered the second quarter of the sixth century, or from 515 to 545 or 550 A.D.

The coins of *Mihir-kul* are of several different types. The silver money is of Sassanian fabric, with the king's head on the obverse and the legend in Indian letters, *Jayatu Mihirkula* or *Jayatu Vrisha-dhwaja*. In front of the face is the *Saiva* standard, the *Vrisha-dhwaja*, a "recumbent bull on the top of the staff." On the *reverse* is a rude fire-altar with two attendants.

The small copper coins which are found in the Eastern Panjâb and in Rajputâna are also of Sassanian type. On the *obverse* is the king's head with the legend in Indian characters *Sri Mihirakula*; on the *reverse* a humped bull with the Indian legend *Jayatu Vrisha*, "May the bull be victorious."

The middle-sized copper coins are copies of the previous Kushân types—the king standing with a spear in left hand, and right hand held downwards over a small altar; legend in Indian letters, *Shâhi Mihira-gula*, or simply *Mihira-kula*; *reverse*, the goddess Lakshmi seated with cornucopiæ.

The large copper coins present the Raja on horseback with the Indian legend *Mihirakula*; *reverse*, the goddess Lakshmi.

With regard to the supposed identity of the Toramâṇas of Eran and Gwalior with the Toramâṇa of Kashmir, which was originally advocated by Rajendradâl and Bhau Dâji, I may say that I cannot conceive it to be possible for the following reasons:—

1. The *Toramâṇa* of Kashmir, according to the *Raja Tarangini*, was never a king, but died in the prison where

he was put by his brother for striking the coins which we now possess. The Scythian Toramâṇa was a powerful king, who ruled over the valley of the Indus, both Panjâb and Sindh, and afterwards conquered Mâlwa, where small silver coins of Gupta type were struck in his name and a colossal boar set up in the first year of his reign. Eventually he left his kingdom to his son Mihirkul, who held it for at least fifteen years.

2. The son of the Kashmir *Toramâṇa* was *Pravarasena*, who is also described as a great conqueror; but if the two Toramâṇas were the same person, then *Pravarasena* must have been *Mihirakula* himself. But there is this difference between the two, that Mihirkul was eventually defeated by Yasodharma, king of Mâlwa, whereas Pravarasena re-established on his throne Sîlâditya, the expelled son of the king of Mâlwa.

3. The coins of Pravarasena, both in gold and silver, show him to have belonged to the *Kidâra* Kushâns, as they present the name of *Kidâra* in beautifully-formed letters written perpendicularly, as on all the Kidarite coins. Lastly, I may observe that the earlier Toramâṇa, like all the White Huns, has his hair cut short, while the Kashmir Toramâṇa has bushy hair like his ancestor *Kidâra*, as copied from the Sassanian kings.

4. I may note also that the characters of the Kashmir coins are of a later date than the others. This is most clearly shown in the attached *â* and *o*, which are simple prolongations of the *mâtras* of the *t* and *m*, instead of marks placed above those letters, as in the *Kyûra* and *Eran* inscriptions of the other Toramâṇa. I note also that the letter *r* has a turn up at the foot on the Kashmir coins of Toramâṇa and his son Pravarasena, which is not found on the others. These differences are clearly shown

in the plate of inscriptions under the head of TORAMÂṆA —A and C.

The great Indian empire of the Hûṇas, under Mihirkul, would appear to have been overthrown by a combined attack of the Hindu princes under Vikramâditya of Mâlwa and Bâlâditya (Nara Sinha Gupta) of Magadha. The scene of his defeat is placed in *Ruma*, in the traditionary account which is attributed to Varâha Mihira, and he is said by Al Beruni to have been killed in his flight "in the region of Karûr, between Multân and the castle of Loni."[9] The castle of Loni is a small fort close to Delhi, which was besieged by Timur, but it is so close to Delhi that the natural description of the position of Karûr would have been between Multân and Delhi. I conjecture the river *Loni*, or the "Salt Stream," was really intended, because it rises in the country of *Ruma*, or the salt district of Sâmbhar, in which the battle is said to have taken place. *Kahrur* is a large town to the west of the Satlej, between Multân and Bahâwalpur. If Mihirkul was defeated near Ajmer in the Ruma country, he would naturally have fled towards the strong fortress of Multân.

TRIBAL NAME.

The first notice of the tribal name of the White Huns of India I take to be the *Ye-po-lo* of the pilgrim Sung-yun, who says that Gandhâra was *formerly* called "the country of *Ye-po-lo*," over which the *Yethas* had placed *Lae-lih* as king two generations before his time.[10] As the king then on the throne had been reigning for at least

---

[9] Sachau's *Albiruni*, ii. 6.

[10] Beal's *Chinese Pilgrims*, I., Introd, p. xcix.

three years, his accession may be fixed about A.D. 515, and that of *Lae-lih* at fifty years earlier, or 465 A.D. I suppose that on this occupation the country was first called after the name of the conquerors *Jabula* (= *Ye-po-lo*), which was either the name or the tribe of *Toramâṇa*, as we learn from the Kyura inscription found in the Salt Range of the Panjâb. In this inscription Toramâṇa is called Mahârâjâ TORAMÂṆA *Shâha Jaüvla*. On my silver coins the name is spelt *Jabubla* and *Jabula*, each preceded by the royal title of *Shâhi*. This at once recalls the name of *Jabun* or *Jabul*, the first king of Multân, who built the temple of the sun.[11] As he was not a Brahman, he must have belonged to the Shâhi dynasty, which preceded the Brahman Chach. As his date is fixed by subtracting the 137 years of the Shâhi dynasty from A.D. 642, the date of Chach's accession, we get A.D. 505 for the accession of *Jabul*, the builder of the temple of the sun, who must therefore be the same person as *Diwaij*, the founder of the Shâhi dynasty in Sindh. But as *Toramâṇa Jabula Shâhi*, the father of Shâhi Mihirkul, was reigning at that very time, I have no hesitation in identifying him with the *Jabula Diwaij* of Multân. To this tribe also I would assign the name of *Zâbulistân* of the early Muhammadan writers. In fact, on several of the later coins of the Ephthalite rulers of Arachosia the name of *Zaülistân* is found in the marginal Pahlavi legends. The people of Zâbulistân spoke a language of their own called *Zâüli*, which was distinct from the *Hiriwi* of Herat, from the *Sakzi* of Sejistan or Sakastan, and from the *Sughdi* of Sughd or Sogdiana.

---

[11] *Elliot's Muhammadan Historians*, by Dowson, i. 205. The name is variously written as *Jabun* and *Jabur*, for which I propose *Jabul*. The change is very slight in Persian characters.

The great power of the White Huns in the countries to the north of the Indian Caucasus lasted for just one century, or from A.D. 455, when they drove Isdegerd II. to the south of the Oxus, down to A.D. 554, when they were subjugated by TUMEN, the Khâkân of the Turks. But they had already established a vast empire over all the countries to the south of the Caucasus, from the shores of the Caspian to the banks of the Satlej, and for a short time even to the banks of the Ganges. The great western extension of their power began with the defeat and death of the Sassanian king, Feroz, in A.D. 483, and lasted until the conquests of the Muhammadans in the eighth century.

The White Huns have been described by Gibbon[12] as "a polite and warlike people, who possessed the commercial cities of Bokhara and Samarkand, who had vanquished the Persian monarch, and carried their victorious arms along the banks, and perhaps to the mouth of the Indus." The doubt of our great historian is now cleared away by the discovery of coins which declare that the White Huns possessed the great cities of Multân and Bahmana in Sindh. From the same source we learn that they also possessed the neighbouring countries of Zâbulistân and Khorasân. The western extension of the Ephthalite dominion to the shores of the Caspian is confirmed by the historian Procopius, who, writing in A.D. 550, states that they held the country to the north of Persia, with *Gorgo* as their capital. As Gorgo or Gurgân was the chief city of Hyrkania, the White Huns must have occupied the whole province of Khorasân. According to Yakut, their capital was *Bâdghîs*, which the Chinese call *Pa-ti-yan* or *Wang-she-ching*, the "town of the king's

12 *Decline and Fall*, c. 42.

house."[13] Their conquest of the country to the south is confirmed by Masudi, who describes *Zâbulistân* as the "kingdom of Firoz," that is, the portion of Persia which was occupied by the *Jabuli* or *Zabuli* tribe of the White Huns.

The historian Gibbon describes the letters in the Scythian character and language which Maniach, prince of the Sogdoites, delivered to Justin II. on the part of Dizabulus, the Khâkân of the Turks, as announcing "a people who had attained the rudiments of science." But as the Turks were an illiterate people, I would ascribe the "Scythian characters" to the cultured Kushâns rather than to the illiterate White Huns, as the Kushâns still formed the bulk of the population of all the countries on the Oxus. In the following century no less than ten of their petty princes claimed descent from the *Shaowu* WEN, the great Kushân conqueror of India, and I believe that Maniach was only one of these tributary chiefs.[14] In A.D. 630, when the pilgrim Hwen Thsang passed through the province occupied by the White Huns (or *Hematala* = *Hephtala*), the population was quite insignificant.[15] It was only three hundred *li* or fifty miles in circuit. The *Varchuni* or White Hun had, in fact, been driven out of the country by Dizabul and his successors.

The kings of the three Indo-Scythian races, the *Tokhari* or Great Kushâns, the *Kidaritæ* or Little Kushâns, and the *Ephthalites* or White Huns, all took the title of Shâhi. The coins of the first, at least all the earlier coins, can be easily recognised; but as the *Kidâras* and the White

---

[13] Edouard Specht, *Études sur l'Asie Centrale—Indo-Scythes et Ephthalites*, p. 24, note 4.

[14] Remusat, *Nouveaux Mélanges Asiatiques*, i. 225; *Kings of Sogdiana*, &c.

[15] Beal's *Chinese Pilgrims*, ii. 290.

Huns were contemporaries from about the middle of the fifth century, there is some difficulty in distinguishing them.

Both peoples adopted the Sassanian types for all their silver coins, and both adhered to the old Kushân types for their copper money. But the White Huns have left no gold coins, while the gold money of the Kidâras of the old Kushân types is very common.

Most of the Ephthalite silver coins are distinguished by a peculiar symbol , which is not found upon any of the known Little Kushân coins, while it occurs on several pieces of the Ephthalite kings, beginning with those of *Jâbula Shâhi*, or *Toramâṇa*. It is also found on my unique coin of *Khinggila*, who was one of the Hûṇa successors of *Mihirkul* as suzerain of Kashmir.

Again, there are two distinct types of legend even in the Indian inscriptions. Thus some coins of Mihirkul give him the simple title of *Sri* preceding the name, whilst others have *jayatu Mihirakula*. Others, again, bear the Scythian form of *Shâhi Mihiragula*.

One peculiarity observable in all the early Ephthalite coins is that the obverse alone has been struck upon one of the current Sassanian coins, and that in consequence the old Sassanian reverse has been nearly obliterated. In many cases the relief of the obverse king's head would appear to have been obtained by punching up from the other side of the coin. This process has left a sunken copy of the head on the reverse.

The question now arises whether any of our numerous Ephthalite coins can be assigned to the "Great Khâkân" of the White Huns, who ruled over the horde in the countries to the north of the Indian Caucasus? As they were an illiterate people, they would almost certainly have adopted the Scytho-Greek alphabet of their predecessors, the Kushâns and Scytho-Sassanians. I possess a few specimens of this description. Two coins of this class from the Hidda Tope were published in *Ariana Antiqua.* The difference did not escape Wilson, who says of one, Pl. XVI. 9 and 10, that "the *peculiar* characters differ from Pahlavi;" and of another, Pl. XVI. 20, that the "characters are *perhaps* intended for Pahlavi."

A single coin in my cabinet, Pl. VII. 2, which is clearly copied from the money of Varahran IV., A.D. 388—399, as the king has a single bird's wing on his head-dress, presents a short legend of two lines in what appear to me to be corrupt Greek characters. The upper line appears to give the title of *Shâhi,* and the lower one looks like ΛIIZOBOΛ, or, by omitting the strokes on the left, simply ZOBOΛ. *Dizabul* or *Shapolio* was the Grand Khâkân of the Turks, whose grandfather had subjugated the White Huns on the Oxus. But his date is perhaps too late, and I rather incline to read *Shâhi Zobol* for *Shâhi Zâbul,* the king of the *Jâbuli* branch of the White Huns—that is, *Toramâṇa Shah Jâbula,* who conquered the Panjâb, Sindh, and Mâlwa about the end of the fifth and the beginning of the sixth century A.D. There are several undoubted coins of this king with Indian characters, which will be mentioned presently.

Amongst Masson's Hidda Tope coins there are two which have debased Greek legends, one of which also has the Ephthalite symbol. Of the first, Wilson gave two specimens (*Ariana Antiqua,* Pl. XVI. 9—10). I have two specimens of this coin, which differ from Masson's in wanting the lunar crescent behind the head. The legends also slightly differ, although they are probably intended for the same.

Of Wilson's second coin (*Ariana Antiqua*, XVI. 20), I have one specimen which has the legend on the left rather more perfect. The head-dress is no longer Sassanian, but appears to be a helmet with flaps or side-pieces. The bust faces the left, and is supported on a double-branched ornament, similar to that on the gems and seals of Shahpur I. The legend seems to be intended for *Shahano Shah Zoobol.* The bust is in very high relief, which has been attained by the very deep repoussé of the reverse.

The only other coins which possess the same apparently Greek legends are smaller in size, and perhaps of somewhat later date. They have the king's bust on the obverse, with various Indian symbols in front of the face. One has the *discus* and *shell* of Vishnu; a second has the *trident* of Siva and *shell* of Vishnu; a third has the *trident* of Siva springing out of a lotus flower. All have the Sassanian fire-altar on the reverse, but always nearly obliterated.

Another class of these smaller coins presents the king on horseback on the obverse, with the same debased Greek legend. The reverse is always very imperfect. On my best specimen there is a large wheel, which may be the *discus* of Vishnu.

Other coins with the king on horseback have Indian legends reading *Shâhi Jabula.* My second specimen seems to read *Shâhi Jaṇabula,* perhaps for *Jam̃bula.* The two coins in the plate are the only specimens of this kind that I have seen. But they are of great interest, as they both bear the Ephthalite symbol, and their Indian legends confirm my readings of the debased Greek legends previously described. The accessory ornaments also are repeated in the *discus* and *shell* of Vishnu of the same pattern as on the bust coins.

The next coins are of peculiar interest, as they point to Kashmir as a portion of the dominions of the Ephthalite king *Jabula* or *Jabuvla*, who is clearly the same as the *Jaüvla* of the inscription of Toramâṇa *Jaüvla* from the Salt Range in the Panjâb. Three of these coins are so much alike in type and size and general fabric that they must almost certainly belong to the same people and the same country. Their legends are—1. *Shâhi Jabuvla;* 2. *Deva Shâhi Khinggila;* 3. *Raja Lakhana* (?) *Udayâditya.* The peculiar name of *Khingkhila* is found in the Raja Tarangini (i. 349) as one of the Rajas of Kashmir closely following *Mihirkul.* As he was also known as *Narendrâdiya*, we learn that these Scythian kings had adopted Indian titles, from which I infer that *Udayâditya* and *Pûrvvâditya* (both meaning "Lord of the East") may be only the titles of other *Scythian* kings of Kashmir. But they were the supreme monarchs of an extensive empire, of which Kashmir was only a tributary province.

There is also a small class of copper coins, which I would assign to *Toramâṇa Jabula.* They bear a king's head of Sassanian aspect on the obverse, and a *chakra*, or *sun-wheel*, on the reverse, with the Indian legend TORA in bold letters. The same legend is found on some of the smaller silver coins, with the name of ZOBOA, or *Jabula.* The same symbol is found also on the Indian copper coins of *Mihirkul*, which bear his name in Indian letters of the Gupta period. It occurs also on a single coin of *Vala* [ditya]. I observe that the peculiar symbol, which is rarely absent from any of the broad silver coins of these Ephthalite kings, does not appear on any of their undoubted Indian coins which are found in the Eastern Panjâb and Rajputâna. A single specimen of the Sun Type, with TORA below (in the cabinet of Mr. Theobald), has a Scythian archer on the obverse. This is certainly a Scythian type (*see* Plate VII. 17).

The silver coins of Mihirkul are exceedingly rare, while his copper coins are not uncommon. The copper coins of the Western Panjâb are all of the Kushân type, with the standing king and seated goddess Lakshmi; but the few silver coins and all the Eastern Panjâb copper pieces bear a Sassanian-looking bust of the king, with the bull and trident of Siva. His devotion to Siva is also strongly marked by the legends of *Jayatu Vrisha-dhwaja* and *Jayatu-Vrisha*. In the Raja Tarangini he is described as a persecutor of Buddhists.

A few copper coins of the Kushân type, with the title of Shâhi, give the names of *Hiranya-kula* and *Jara*. The latter name seems to be incomplete, but four coins of different issues offer nothing further. On one of these the goddess Lakshmi is seated on a *Sinhâsan*, or "lion-throne." These coins I would assign to Gândhâra.

The coins from Pl. VIII. 14 to Pl. IX. 13 nearly all present the Ephthalite symbol, and all save one have Indian legends. The names of *Bhârana* or *Jârana* and *Triloka*, the titles of *Pûrvvâditya* and *Deva-Shâhi*, are all clear enough, and so is the legend of *Jayatu Sri Narendra* on the two copper coins Pl. IX. 12 and 13. But all that can be said about them is, that they must have flourished during the sixth and seventh centuries in the countries bordering upon India, or even in North-West India itself.

After these I have brought together all the latest specimens which bear the Ephthalite symbol. Some of them have Indian legends, of which the most remarkable is No. 16. I read it as *Jayatu Bayâr Khotalan*. A district named *Khotalan* is to the north of the Caucasus. The coins Nos. 18 and 19, which bear native legends, present exactly the same head as on Nos. 20, 21, and 22, which have the simple Indian legend *Sri Shâhi.* I infer, therefore, that the native legend must give the equivalent of *Sri Shâhi.* The latter part of it certainly seems to read *Shono* in debased Greek letters. In support of this reading I may refer to a crystal seal in my possession, with the Indian legend *Shânê* on the left side, and the debased Greek *Shaono* on the right.[16] The coin (Pl. X. 2) bears exactly the same legend as that on Figs. 3 and 4. It is Pahlavi, which Mr. Thomas read as *Nipki Malka.* I prefer *Napki* as the name, and I would ascribe these coins to the king of *Kipin* (or Kophene = Arakhosia), who is mentioned by the Chinese as wearing "un bonnet fait en tête de bœuf."[17] The coins in the plate, Nos. 3 and 4, which present a buffalo's head surmounting the king's head-dress, seem to correspond with this description; but the same name is found on No. 2, which has a simple head-dress surmounted by three tridents or *trisuls.* These coins apparently belong to the middle of the seventh century. Ghazni was the capital of Kipin.

The coins in Plate X., Nos. 5—11, are all bilingual or trilingual, the various legends being in Indian *Nâgari,* Persian *Pahlavi,* and some unknown Scythian characters. Figs. 5 and 6 present a short Indian inscription of two lines on the reverse, which is so imperfectly formed that it has hitherto baffled all attempts to decipher it. It begins with *Sri.*

Fig. 7 has also a short *Nâgari* inscription of two lines, which was read by Wilson as *Sri Bahmana Vâsu Deva.*

---

[16] *Numismatic Chronicle,* 1893. Pl. X. 1.

[17] Remusat, *Nouveaux Mélanges Asiatiques,* i. 211.

The word read as *Bahmana* is uncertain, but I can suggest nothing better. I believe that it refers to the famous capital of Sindh called *Bâhmanwâsi* by the Hindus, and afterwards *Brâhmanâbâd* by the Muhammadans. It was the "city of Brahmans" of Alexander's historians. Vâsu Deva must have been the king of Sindh. The marginal legends on both sides are in Scythian characters.

The remaining coins of Plate X. are remarkable as presenting the same bust on the reverse, which many years ago I identified with the famous "sun-god" of Multân, as the head is rayed. With these I compare a coin of Khusru II. Parvez of Persia, dated in the year 37 of his reign, or A.D. 628. In the native histories he is said to have invaded territories of the Indian king, who fell in battle against him. I conjecture that this coin may have been struck to commemorate this victory.

No. 9 coin has long been known for its trilingual inscriptions. Two specimens were obtained by Ventura in the great Stûpa of Mânikyâla. The principal inscription is the marginal legend of the obverse in the Indian language and Nâgari letters. On the same side, in front of the face, there is a short legend in Scythian characters. The legends on the reverse are all in Persian Pahlavi. A large number of these coins have been found in different places on both sides of the Indus. Two specimens were obtained by Ventura in the Mânikyâla Stûpa. Dr. Lord got forty to the north of the Caucasus. I have received some twenty or thirty from Kabul, and I am aware that a few have been found in Sindh and Kacch. The letters of the Nâgari legend vary a little in some of the shapes, but my reading of the whole legend agrees substantially with that of James Prinsep. Thomas made one important suggestion in the reading of *Shâhi* for Prinsep's *Vâhi.* I give their two readings for comparison with my own :—

Prinsep—*Sri hitivira Airâna cha paramesuara Sri Vahitigân devajânita.*
Thomas—*Sri hitivira kharala cha parameswara Sri Shâhitina devanârita.*
Author—*Sri Hitivi cha Airân cha parameswara Sri Shâhi-Tigin Devajârita.*

I have seen a great number of these coins, and I still possess twenty-six specimens. I am now able to say decidedly that the name of the king is *Tigin,* the *gi* being very clear on several of my coins. *Shâhi* is the well-known Scythian title for "king"; and *Devajâ,* or "son of heaven," was an Indian title adopted by Scythians as well as by Sassanians. The Pahlavi legends on the reverse have been read by Thomas as follows :—

To left, *Saf-Tansaf-Tef ;* to right, *Takân Khorasân Malkâ.*

For *Tansaf* I propose to read *Takhif,* thus making *Saf Takhif Tef* the equivalent of *Shâhi Tagina Deva.* Similarly I take *Takân Khorasân Malkâ* to be the equivalent of *Hitivi cha Airân parameswara,* the "king of India and Persia." *Tâkan* or *Tâki* was the name of the Panjâb, with its capital cities of *Tâki-shahr* or Taxila, Sâkala or Sangala, and Multân. The name of the king was preserved in the famous city of *Takînâbâd* on the Helmand, which, according to the Tabakât-i-Nâsiri, was the largest town in Garmsir. It is noticed by Nâsir-uddin-Tûsi and Ulug Beg under the erroneous name of *Takniâbâd* by the misplacement of the points. The Tabakât-i-Nasiri has *Takînâbâd.*

The possession of Khorâsân and Zâbulistân by the White Huns dates from the defeat and death of the

Sassanian king Firoz in A.D. 483, when the conquerors took possession of those provinces and made *Gorgo* (Gurgân) their capital. Upwards of three centuries later, when the country was visited by Masudi, Zâbulistân was still known as the "kingdom of Firoz." As the head-dress of *Shâhi Tagîn* is a simple tiara surmounted by a lion's head, he must be placed before the time of Khusru II. Parvez. I would therefore identify him with *Diwâij II.*, the *Shâhi-shâhin* of the Chach-Nâma, and I would fix his reign to about 565 to 595 A.D.

The next coin of this class, No. 10 of the plate, bears the name of the king *Sri Vâsu Deva* in Indian characters, with several Pahlavi legends on both sides. The first step in reading these difficult legends was made by Olshausen. A further advance was made by Thomas, who succeeded in finding the name of the king *Vâsu Deva*, in the Pahlavi *Varsu Tef*; but the decipherment of the whole is still incomplete. His readings were:—

OBVERSE { Left, *Afzût* (= increase); right, *Saf Varsu Tef.*
Margin, *Pun-shami dât* (In nomine justi judicis).
Saf Varsao Tef-Wahman ach Multân malkâ.

REVERSE { Left, *Panchai Zâülistân*; right, *Sri Vâsu Deva.*
Margin (not read).

Thomas felt some doubt about the reading of *Panchai* on the left reverse. I differ from his reading, as the first letter is T, and not P. I read the word as *Tukân* in conjunction with *Zâülistân*, and I believe it to be intended for the Panjâb or *Tâkan*, of which *Tâki-shahr*, or Taxila, was the capital. Of the reverse marginal legend I cannot make anything certain. I read doubtfully *Sapardalakshân* for *Sapâdalaksha* or Rajputâna (Sawâlak).

The coins of Vâsu Deva are still very scarce, only six specimens being known to me. The king's head-dress is a direct copy of the double-winged crown of Khusru Parvez, and the coins have the same crescents and stars in the margin. As the ruler of Multân and the contemporary of Parvez, I incline to identify him with Rai Siharas of Sindh, who was attacked by the king of Nimroz or Sejistan and killed in battle, apparently on the frontier of Mekrân. If the coin of Khusru Parvez with the Multân sun-god on the reverse was struck on this occasion, the date on the coin, the year 37 of his reign, or A.D. 628, would be also the date of Vâsu Deva's death.

The last king of Sindh, called Rai Sâhasi, was the son of the opponent of Parvez. In the British Museum there is a unique copper coin of the sun-god type which I would attribute to this king. It has the same double-winged head-dress, but the legends appear to be partly in Scythian characters and partly in Pahlavi. The margins on both sides are occupied by the Scythian legends, which are at present quite unintelligible. But in the two Pahlavi legends of the reverse I read on the left of the head *Sapardalakshân*, and to the right *Zâülistân*.

Sapâdalaksha, or "one lakh and a quarter," was the old name of Rajputâna. The shortened form was *Sawalakh*, which is still preserved in the present form of *Sawâlik*. The early Muhammadan writers describe *Mandor*, the old capital of Mârwâr, as being in Sawâlik. Ajmer also was in it, and Hânsi is specially mentioned as the capital of Sawâlik. The name is said to have been derived from the great number of scattered hills in the country, for which 125,000 is a significant expression. Sapâdalaksha is mentioned as the territory of King Asoka-balla in my Buddha Gayâ inscriptions of the twelfth century, before the Muhammadan occupation.

Our knowledge of the early history of Sindh prior to

the Muhammadan conquest is derived from two native histories, the *Chach-Nâma* and the Tuhfat al Kirâm. The Chach-Nâma was originally written in Arabic to record the conquest of Sindh by the Arabs under Muhammad Kâsim in A.D. 713, but only a Persian translation now exists. The work must have been written before A.D. 753, as there is no mention of the Muhammadan city of Mansûra, which was founded during the reign of the Khalif Al Mansûr. It is therefore almost a contemporary record of the conquest, which transferred the possession from Râja Dâhir, the son of the Brahman Raja Chach, to the Muhammadans. It begins with a brief notice of the three kings of the Rai dynasty who preceded Chach. The Tuhfat al Kirâm gives two additional reigns, and states that the reigns of the five Rais lasted for 137 years.

For the accession of Chach we possess two statements, which agree in fixing it not earlier than 641 A.D. The first is the length of the two reigns of Chach and his son Dahir, or 40 + 33 lunar years = 73 lunar years or 71 solar years, and as Dahir was killed on the 11th Ramzân A.H. 93, or 21st June 712 A.D., the accession of Chach must have taken place in 712—71 = 641 A.D. The second authority is the statement of the pilgrim Hwen Thsang that when he visited Sindh in September 641 A.D., the ruler was a *Shu-to-lo* or Sudra. At that time, therefore, the last king of the Rai dynasty was still reigning. Deducting 137 years from 642, we get 505 A.D. as the date of the accession of the Rai dynasty. The following list gives the names of the kings of the Rai dynasty, with the names derived from coins for comparison—all of them had the title of Shâhi-shâh. Their rule was not confined to the province of Sindh, but embraced all the neighbouring countries up to the frontiers of Kirmân on the west, up to the foot of the Kashmir hills on the north, and up to the boundary of the kingdom of Kanauj on the east. These limits were maintained to the last, as I find that Chach went to Mekrân to settle the boundary of *Kirmân* with Persia, and to Shâkalhâ or Sâkala to settle the boundary with *Kashmir*. On the east the ruler of *Chitrâwar* or Chitor is said to have been a relative and ally of Rai Sâhasi. The Indian dominions of the Ephthalites formed a mighty empire, the rival of Persia both in power and wealth.

A.D.	*Tuhfat-al-Kirâm.*	*Chach-Nâma.*	Coins.
505	Rai Diwâij I.		Shâhi Jabubal = TORAMÂNA.
535	Rai Siharas.		Shâhi Mihirgul = GOLLAS.
565	Rai Sâhasi.	Rai Diwâij II.	Shâhi Tigin Devaja.
595	Rai Siharas II.	Rai Siharas.	—— Vâsu Deva.
627	Rai Sâhasi II.	Rai Sâhasi.	—— —— ? name not read.

The ancient title of the Ephthalite kings was *Tsanyu* or *Chanyu*, which was changed for *Khâkân*, or χαγάνος as written by the Greeks. But just like the Sassanian kings, who call themselves by the foreign title of *Malkân-malkâ* instead of by their native one of Shâhân Shâh, so these White Huns preferred the Kushân and Indian titles of Shâhi and Maharaja to their own title of Khâkân. Both Toramâṇa and his son Mihirkul, who were certainly White Huns, take the title of Maharaja and Shâhi written in Indian characters.

About the middle of the sixth century A.D. the White Huns were conquered by Muhan Khan, the chief of the great Turkish horde, who sent an embassy to Constantinople under Maniach, Prince of the Sogdoites. His letter in the Scythian character and language was received by

Justin in 569 A.D. A return embassy was sent by Tiberius in 582; but on its arrival in 584, they found that the Emperor *Shapelo* or *Disabul* was dead. In 588 his successor, *Shahu Khan*, sent a letter to the Emperor Maurice. As Prince of the Sogdoites, Maniach must have been only a tributary chief, either a Kushân or an Ephthalite; his letter in the Scythian character must have been in the corrupted Greek characters which were common to both. As late as the ninth century the ruler of Mawarunnahr is called king of the Kushâns by Khordâdbah.

Unfortunately, we have no coins that can be certainly attributed to the Ephthalite kings of the Oxus. The coins with the  symbol, which I believe to belong to the White Huns, may be divided into two classes:—

1. Those with legends in unknown characters.
2. Those with legends in Indian letters.

Specimens of each kind were found together by Masson in No. 10 Hidda Tope. Similarly, in a parcel of about eighty of these Scytho-Sassanian coins that came to me together, I found some of each kind. The only difference that I could perceive was in a few specimens of No. 1 class, which were certainly of earlier date than any of the No. 2 class; I refer particularly to *Ariana Antiqua*, Plate XVI. Figs. 9 and 10, on which the king's head-dress is copied from the Sassanian coins of Sapor III., A.D. 383—388. The characters look like debased Greek; they are certainly not Pahlavi or Indian. A single coin with the winged head-dress of Varahran IV., A.D. 420—440, has similar characters, which might be read by taking the two lines, Boustrophedon fashion, as *Sholono-Bozino* for *Shulo-pachin*, the famous *Khush-nawâz* of Persian history, who defeated the Sassanian Firoz in A.D. 482. He is called *Fizun* by Firdausi.

These coins I would assign to the northern branch of Ephthalites on the Oxus, as I believe that the debased Greek characters had already been given up by the southern branch of the Ephthalites on the Indus. The earliest certain coins of the Indian Ephthalites are the silver pieces of Toramâṇa and his son Mihirkul, both of whom take the title of *Shâhi* instead of *Khâkân*. The coins of Udayâditya and Khinggila belong to the same period.

Since writing this paper, I have found a direct proof that the Sâhasi kings of Sindh were White Huns. Elliot[18] quotes Khâki Shirâzi, who says: "In the year 22 the province of Sejistan was conquered . . , and in the same year Makrân was subdued. . . . The ruler of that province, whose name in the language of the country was *Zambil*, was also ruler of *Sind*." The year A.H. 22 began on 30th November A.D. 642. The conquest of Chach Brahman may therefore have taken place in A.D. 643. Vivien St. Martin assigns it to 644 A.D. Perhaps it is this *Zambil*, ruler of Sind, who is referred to by Masudi (Elliot II., 418), as the "Prince, named Ranbil, who reigned in the *valley of the Indus*, and who, after subjugating E. Persia, advanced to the banks of the Tigris and Euphrates."

This name of *Zambil* is only another variant of the *Zanbil, Zanbol, Ranbil, Ranbol*, &c., which is given to the kings of Kabul and Sistan by all the early Muhammadan writers. One of my coins with the horseman obverse has *Janbula* in Nâgari letters. This is, of course, the true Indian form of the Scythian *Zanbol* or Zabul, as the Indian alphabets have no *z*.

---

[18] *Muhammadan Historians*, ii. 418.

COINS OF THE WHITE HUNS.

PLATE VII.

No.	Metal.	Wt. Grs.	UNASSIGNED ZABULI COINS.
1	Æ	60	Author, 2 coins; *Ariana Antiqua*, xvi. 10, from Hidda Tope. Head of king to right; Sassanian head-dress like Sapor II.; Ephthalite symbol in front of face. Legend in unread characters. *Rev.*—Indistinct remains of fire altar and attendants. N.B.—Nearly all of the Ephthalite coins have been Sassanian pieces restruck only on the obverse side, which has nearly obliterated the reverse original.
2	Æ	49	Author, unique, copied from money of Varahran IV. Head of king to right, with wing on head-dress. Legend in corrupt Greek letters, perhaps intended to represent *Shoono Zobol.* *Rev.*—Indistinct remains of fire altar and attendants.
3	Æ	55	Author, *Ariana Antiqua*, xvi. 20. Head of king to left, with tall helmet; trident before face. To left, some unread characters; to right, in corrupt Greek characters, ÞAO ZOBOΛ = *Shao Zobol.* *Rev.*—Indistinct remains of fire altar and attendants. H. H. Wilson, *Ariana Antiqua*, p. 399, suggests that the characters are perhaps intended for Pahlavi. He notices that all these coins are of rude fabric, and slightly concave on the reverse, which is always very indistinct.
4	Æ	50	Author, 0·95 inch. Beardless head of king to right, with crescent on front of head-dress; a jewelled circle

PLATE VII. No.	Metal.	Wt. Grs.	
			and a shell to right. Legend in corrupt Greek letters, × × ZOBOΛ. *Rev.*—Indistinct fire altar.
5	Æ	52	Author, 0·90 inch. Beardless head of king to right, with crescent; trident and shell to right. Remains of corrupt Greek legend, same as on No. 4. *Rev.*—Indistinct.
6	Æ	55	Author, 0·85 inch. Horseman to right, with crescent on helmet; large shell to right. Remains of Greek legend, same as No. 4. *Rev.*—Indistinct. Remains of Indian legend clear, *yatu* (Jayatu). N.B.—These three coins I suppose to belong to the Zabuli tribe of White Huns before their occupation of the Kabul Valley. Or they may belong to *Lae-lih*, the leader of the expedition to the south of the Indian Caucasus. The coins still bear the corrupt Greek characters, but as they also bear the shell of Vishnu and the trident of Siva, they show some connection with India. Their date would be about 560 to 590 A.D.
7	Æ	55	Author, 0·85 inch; a plated coin. See *Prinsep's Antiquities*, xxxiii. Fig. 1. Horseman to right, crescent on helmet, Ephthalite symbol to right. Legend unread, but may be corrupt Greek beginning with ZOBOΛA to left. Prinsep's coin has the symbol behind the horse. *Rev.*—Large ornamental wheel; traces of *Jayatu* in Indian letters. N.B.—I have two other specimens: *One* like Prinsep's, with vase in front of horse, and traces of *Jayatu* on reverse. The *other* with a *shell* in front of horse, and *yatu* (*Jayatu*) very distinct. This Indian word in Indian letters connects these horseman coins with India.

PLATE VII. No.	Metal.	Wt. Grs.	
			SHAHI—JABUL OR JAMBUL.
8	Æ	53	Author, 0·90 inch; unique. King on horseback to right; *shell over horse's* head, with star above. Behind the king the Ephthalite symbol. Indian legend, *Shahi Jabûla.* *Rev.*—Fire altar with an attendant on each side.
9	Æ	50·5	Author, 0·80 inch; unique. King on horseback to right, with crescent on helmet; club over head of horse; Ephthalite symbol behind king. Indian legend, *Shahi Janbûla.* *Rev.*—Fire altar with two attendants; very rude.
			SHAHI JABUVLA.
10	Æ	56	Author, 1·0 inch; unique. Other specimens differ. Beardless head of king to right, with crescent on front of helmet; large earring. Indian legend to right, *Shâhi Jabuvlah.* *Rev.*—Indistinct, the coin being *repoussé.*
13	Æ	50·5	Author, 1·10 inch. Three or four other specimens in poor condition. Beardless head of king to right, with crescent on helmet; large crescent behind shoulders; club in front of face; Ephthalite symbol behind. Indian legend behind head, *Shahi* (written reversely) *Jabula* (written direct). *Rev.*—Indistinct.
			DEVA SHAHI KHINGGILA.
11	Æ	48	Author, 1·05 inch, unique. Beardless head of king to right; crescent on helmet; large crescent behind shoulders; long earrings; ornamental wheel before face; Ephthalite symbol behind head. Indian legend, *Deva Shahi Khinggila.* *Rev.*—Indistinct.

PLATE VII. No.	Metal.	Wt. Grs.	
			N.B.—In the *Raja Tarangini* [i. 352] a king named *Khingkhila* is mentioned amongst the successors of *Mihirakula*. As he was also called *Narendrâditya*, which is an Indian name, *Khinggila* must have been his Ephthalite name. The general appearance of his bust corresponds almost exactly with that of *Jabula*, who was the father of *Mihirakula*.
			RAJA LAKHANA(?) UDAYÂDITYA.
12	AR	57	Author, 1·10 inch. Three other specimens: one, Mr. Theobald; two, E. Thomas in Prinsep I. 411. Beardless head of king to right, similar to the heads of *Jabula* and *Khinggila;* crescent on helmet, and small earring in ear; Ephthalite symbol missing. Indian legend, *Raja Lakhana*(?) *Udayâditya.* *Rev.*—Indistinct. N.B.—Thomas proposes to read *Lamata*, and suggests the kingdom of *Lumghan*; but I prefer to take *Udayâditya* as the Indian title of the foreign king *Lakhana*, as in the example of *Narendrâditya* for *Khinggila.*
14	AR	59	} Author, 1·15 inch; selected from eight or ten specimens. See *Ariana Antiqua*, xvi. 19.
15	AR	60	} Beardless head of king to right; crescent on helmet; *chauries* (or tufts of feathers, as Wilson suggests) spring from the shoulders; Ephthalite symbol in front of face. Legend on No. 14 unread. Legend on No. 15 in corrupt Greek written from right to left, *Shoho* = *Shâhi.* N.B.—Wilson notes that Masson's coins were found in the great Tope at Hidda, and that great numbers of them are met with at Begrâm. I was informed that most of my coins of this and similar classes were found in Stûpas—especially the coins like Plate IX. Fig. 1—and most of the other coins in the same Plate. A few of my coins were purchased at the sale of the remains of the Masson collection in London.

PLATE VII.

No.	Metal.	Wt. Grs.	
16	Æ	57	Author, see *Prinsep's Antiquities*, by E. Thomas, Pl. XXXIII. 15, 16. Bare head of king to right in circle of beads. Indian letter *Bu* to right. *Rev.*—Solar symbol above. Indian legend, *To* below in large letters.
17	Æ	57	Mr. Theobald. Archer standing with bow in his left hand. *Rev.*—Same as No. 1, with *To* below in large letters. N.B.—The syllable *To* is supposed to be intended for TORAMANA. The assignment is suggested by the fact that the small copper coins of Mihirakula bear the same solar symbol. *Prinsep's Antiquities*, by E. Thomas, Pl. XXXIV. 17. Male figure standing to front, holding spear in left hand. *Rev.*—Solar symbol as on No. 1, with Indian letters below, *Shuta*.
18	Æ	26	Author, unique. Bare head of king to right. *Rev.*—Solar symbol above, as on No. 2. Indian legend below, *Sri Vala* + + + .

PLATE VIII.

SHAHI MIHIRAKULA.

No.	Metal.	Wt. Grs.	
1	Æ	57	Author, see *Prinsep's Antiquities*, by E. Thomas, Pl. XXXIV., Figs. 1, 2, 4, 5. Beardless head of king to right. Indian legend, *Sri Mihira-kula*. *Rev.*—Humped bull to left. Indian legend, *Jayatu Vṛisha*. N.B.—Prinsep read *Maharaja* ; E. Thomas read *Mahârakusa*.
2	Æ	48	Author, see Prinsep, by E. Thomas, Pl. XXXIV. Fig. 3. Head of king as on No. 5. Same legend, *Sri Mihira-kula*.

PLATE VIII. No.	Metal.	Wt. Grs.	
			Humped Bull with legend above, *Jayatu Vrisha.*
3	AR	36·5	British Museum, from Abbott collection; E. Thomas in Prinsep, i. p. 411. Beardless head of king to right, with crescent on front of head-dress; bull standard in front of face, trident behind head. Indian legend, *Jayatu Mihirakula.* *Rev.*—Remains of fire altar and attendants nearly obliterated. E. Thomas published this coin in *Prinsep's Antiquities*, i. p. 411, but he failed to read the name.
4	AR	56	Author, 2 coins, but duplicate in poor condition. Beardless head of king to right, as on No. 3. Bull standard before face, and trident behind head. Indian legend, *Jayatu Vrisha-dhwaja.* *Rev.*—Fire altar with attendant on each side, quite distinct.
5	Æ	121	Author, 5 specimens. Standing figure of king to left, as on the Kushân coins. Indian legend, *Shâhi Mihiragula.* The *gula* is quite distinct on all the coins, and I note that this form of the name is used with the title *Shâhi.* *Rev.*—Seated goddess with cornucopiæ, as on the Kushân coins. N.B.—The Indian letter *G* has the same curved limb to the left as is used in the inscription of Toramâṇa Shâhi from the Kyura Salt Mines.
6	Æ	109	Author. King standing to front with spear in left hand; star in field to left. Indian legend written reversed, *Mihira-kula.* *Rev.*—Seated goddess with cornucopiæ. Star above on right.

PLATE VIII.

No.	Metal.	Wt. Grs.	
7	Æ	110	Author, 5 specimens, 0·90 inch. King on horseback to right. Indian legend reversed [*Mihi*]*rakula*. *Rev.*—Seated goddess as on the Kushân coins.
			SHAHI JABULA[?].
8	Æ	59	Author, unique, copper plated. Beardless head of king with crescent on front of helmet. Indian legend rude, read conjecturally, *Shâhi Jabula.* *Rev.*—Remains of fire altar and attendants.
			HIRANYA-KULA.
9	Æ	124	Author, 5 specimens. King standing to left holding spear in left hand. Indian legend, *Shâhi* [*Hi*]*ranya-kula.* *Rev.*—Seated goddess as on Kushân coins.
10	Æ	126	Author. King as on No. 9. Indian legend [*Hira*]*nya-kula Shâhi.* *Rev.*—Seated goddess.
			SHAHI-JARA[?].
11	Æ	122	Author, unique. Half-length figure of king to left, with right hand placed on his waist. Indian legend, *Shâhi Jara.* *Rev.*—Seated goddess.
12	Æ	118	Author. Standing figure of king holding spear in left hand, as on Kushân coins. Indian legend *Shâhi Jari.* *Rev.*—Seated goddess with cornucopiæ.
13	Æ	105	British Museum. Author, 2 specimens, 105 and 104 grains. King seated on a *Sinhâsan*, or "Lion throne"; lion's head to right. In king's left hand a trident; in his right hand an indistinct object. Indian legend, *Shâhi Jara.*

PLATE VIII. No.	Metal.	Wt. Grs.	
			Rev.—Goddess on "Lion throne," with cornucopiæ in left hand and uncertain object in right hand. N.B.—I have 5 plated coins [Pl. IX. Fig. 3] on which I read the Indian legend, *Jayatu Bhâraṇa*, but with some hesitation, as the name may also be read *Jâraṇa*; and these may be the silver money of Sassanian type with fire altar, of which Fig. 13 above is the copper currency. The silver coins generally take the Sassanian type, while the copper coins adhere to the Kushân type.
14	Æ	58	Author, 2 specimens. Beardless head of king to right with small earring and helmet; crescent behind head; Ephthalite symbol in front. Legend to right in unknown characters. *Rev.*—Fire altar and attendants nearly obliterated.
15	Æ	54	Author, 2 specimens. Beardless head of king to right; crescent in front of helmet. Bust placed on a large crescent; shell in front of face; Ephthalite symbol behind head. Indian legend, *Shâhi* to left, and *Shâhi* repeated to right. *Rev.*—Fire altar, indistinct.
16	Æ	49	Author, 3 specimens. Beardless head of king to right, as on No. 15; crescent in front of helmet. Bust placed on large crescent; club in front of face; Ephthalite symbol behind. *Shâhi* to right and *Shâhi* to left, as on No. 15. *Rev.*—Fire altar, indistinct.
17	Æ	50	Author, 7 specimens, with slight differences. Beardless head of king with crescent on helmet; earring in ear; ornamental circle in front of face; Ephthalite symbol behind head. Indian legend of two letters, *Bugo* or *Buto*. *Rev.*—Fire altar with flames; remains of attendants.

PLATE IX.

No	Metal.	Wt. Grs.	
1	Æ	52	Author. See *Ariana Antiqua*, xvi. 8, p. 395, from "Hidda Tope." Beardless head of king to right, with small earring. Ephthalite symbol to left. Indian legend to right, *Vaiga* or *Vanga*. *Rev.*—Fire altar with two attendants.
			BHÂRAṆA OR JÂRAṆA.
2	Æ	50	Author, copper plated, five or six specimens.
3	Æ	42	Beardless head of king to right, with small earring. Trisul in front of head-dress; hand in front of face holding flower. Indian legend, *Jayatu Bhâraṇa*, or *Jâraṇa*. Shell behind head. *Rev.*—Fire altar with attendants. N.B.—See the copper coins, Plate VIII., 11, 12, 13, of *Shâhi Jâra*, which I have suggested as the copper money of this king, *Jâraṇa*.
4	Æ	50	Author, unique. Beardless head of king to left, with crescent on helmet. Indian legend, *Jayatu Raku* × *Sr* +. Name doubtful. *Rev.*—Fire altar, nearly obliterated.
5	Æ	55	Author. See *Prinsep's Antiquities*, by E. Thomas, XXXIII. 4, for a similar coin. Beardless head of king to right, with crescent in front of helmet. Small human figure with raised hand before face. Indian legend, *Saha*, to left, *Shâhi* to right. [A coin in the British Museum with a similar small figure has the letters, *ditya*, *Prinsep* I. 410.] *Rev.*—Remains of fire altar. N.B.—Prinsep's coin has the Indian letters *Pati* instead of *Shâhi*.
			TRILOKA.
6	Æ	44	Author; four plated coins; intended for silver.

PLATE IX. No.	Metal.	Wt. Grs.	
			Beardless head of king to right, with crescent on helmet. Ephthalite symbol to right, and Indian legend, *Triloka*. *Rev.*—Fire altar, nearly obliterated.
			PURVVÂDITYA.
7	Æ	53	Author, very rare. See E. Thomas in *Prinsep*, I., p. 411. Beardless head of king to right, with crescent in front of helmet; double drop earring. In front, wheel on lotus throne. Ephthalite symbol behind head. Indian legend to right, *Purvvâditya*. *Rev.*—Fire altar, almost obliterated. E. Thomas has misread the legend as *Pûrmaditya*.
8	Æ	55	Author. Beardless head of king, with crescent in front of helmet. In front of face, vessel on stand holding a three-branched symbol, perhaps a trisul. Traces of letters above. *Rev.*—Fire altar, nearly obliterated.
9	Æ	53	Author. Bearded head of king, with crescent in front of helmet; trisul in front of face. Ephthalite symbol behind. Indian legend, *Deva Shâhi*. *Rev.*—Fire altar, nearly obliterated.
10	Æ	58	Author, unique. Beardless head of king to right, with crescent in front of helmet, and earring in ear with two strings of pearls. Large flower on undulated stem before face. Indian legend to right, *Shâhi*. *Rev.*—Fire altar, nearly obliterated.
11	Æ	52	Author, unique. Beardless head of king to right, with crescent in front of helmet; trident in front of face, and nondescript object behind

PLATE IX. No.	Metal.	Wt. Grs.	
			head. Indian legend, *Shâhi* × × *na Shâhi*. *Rev.*—Indistinct remains of fire altar.
			NARENDRA.
12	Æ	51	Author, 9 specimens. Beardless head of king to right; earring with two drops; winged head-dress with crescent between; shell behind. Indian legend, *Jayatu Sri Narendra.* *Rev.*—Square fire altar, with two attendants; object below like a pair of spectacles upside down. N.B.—A poor specimen with the king's head has an ornamental wheel on reverse.
13	Æ	57	Author, 2 specimens. King seated to front, right hand on hip, left hand holding sceptre. *Rev.*—Seated goddess, holding flower in left hand. Indian legend written reversed, *Jayatu Sri Narendra.*
			The following are other varieties of Ephthalite coinage. *Ariana Antiqua*, Pl. XVII. 20. Head of king; copied from Sassanian coin. Ephthalite symbol. *Ariana Antiqua*, Pl. XVII. 21. Head of king, with crescent. Trident. Indian legend, *Shâhi.*
14	Æ	48	Author; *Ariana Antiqua*, XVI. 18. Beardless head of king to right, with tall helmet, and two drops of earring. Indian legend to left in large, well-formed letters, *Shâhi.* Wilson, *Ariana Antiqua*, p. 399, has mistaken one of these letters for the Ephthalite symbol. *Rev.*—Fire altar, with two attendants.
15	AR	52	Author, unique. Beardless head of king to right, with high helmet. Altar with three-branched flower to right; Ephthalite symbol to

PLATE IX. No.	Metal.	Wt. Grs.	
			left. Indian legend apparently reversed; read from right to left, *Maboma Shâhi.* *Rev.*—Fire altar, nearly obliterated.
16	Æ	56	Author, 2 coins. Beardless head of king to right, with crescent in front of helmet; to right, altar, as on No. 15; to left, modified Swastika. *Jayatu Bayâr Khotalaṇ.* *Rev.*—Fire altar, nearly obliterated.
17	Æ	44	Author, 11 specimens. Beardless head of king to right, with crescent in front of helmet. On shoulders, two crescents, with an upright middle stroke; hand extended before face holding flower; club behind head. *Rev.*—Remains of fire altar and attendants.
			NAPKI MALKA.
18	Æ	52	Author, 12 specimens. Beardless head of king to right, with trisul in middle of crescent on forehead. Ephthalite symbol behind head. Legend in corrupt Greek letters = *Sio Shono* (or *Shoho*) = *Sri Shâhi.*
19	Æ	49	Author. Two similar coins with countermark on neck, *Tiri*, in Indian letters. Ephthalite symbol behind head. Three similar coins with insect as a countermark.
20	Æ	46	Author; has been plated; see *Ariana Antiqua*, XXI. 22. Similar head of king, with flag in front of face. Ephthalite symbol behind. Legend in Indian letters, *Sri Shâhi.* *Rev.*—Fire altar, distinct, with attendants.
21	Æ	41	Author; copper thickly plated. Same types and legend as No. 20, without flag. See *Ariana Antiqua*, XVII. 11.
22	Æ	28	Author. Same types and legend as No. 21.

PLATE IX.

No.	Metal.	Wt. Grs.	
23	Æ	26	Author, unique. Beardless head of king to right, with two crescents and trisuls on head-dress, holding flower in right hand before face. Indian legend, *Sri Shâhi*. *Rev.*—Indistinct. With these coins may be compared a crystal gem in the possession of the author. (*Num. Chron.* 1893, Pl. X. 1.) King's head to right, beardless. A two-drop earring. Indian legend to left, *Shânê*. Corrupt Greek to right, *Shaono*.
24	Æ	47	Author. Small thick coin. Beardless head of king, with triple crescent and trisul head-dress. Ephthalite symbol behind. To right Pahlavi legend of two letters, *KI*. *Rev.*—Fire altar and attendants.

PLATE X.

No.	Metal.	Wt. Grs.	
1	Æ	51	Author; broad thin coin; unique. Same types as IX. 24, and same legend and Ephthalite symbol. The king holds out a flower in his right hand.
2	Æ	51	Author, 13 specimens. Same types as IX. 24, with modified Ephthalite symbol, and Pahlavi legend, *Napki Malka*.
3	Æ	51	Author, 25 specimens, several plated; *Ariana Antiqua*, XVII. 5-7—XXI. 21. See *Prinsep's Antiquities*, by E. Thomas, XXXIII. 3. Beardless head of king; head-dress surmounted by a buffalo's head, and with wings. Pahlavi legend to right, *Napki Malik*. *Rev.*—Fire altar, with two attendants; an ornamental wheel over each attendant's head; two letters to left, which look like Indian; one to right, Gandharian *I*.

PLATE X.

No.	Metal.	Wt. Grs.	
4	Æ	41	Author, same type as No. 3, but king's head larger, and his cropped hair very con spicuous. Pahlavi legend as No. 3; Pahlavi A to left. *Rev.*—Similar to No. 3. N.B.—The Chinese annals record that the king of Kipin in the seventh century A.D. wore "*un bonnet fait en tête de bœuf.*" [Remusat, *Nouveaux Mélanges Asiatiques*, I., 211.]
5	Æ	50	Author, 5 specimens; *Ariana Antiqua*, XVII. 6. Beardless head of king, with two wings and two trisuls in head-dress, and a small earring. Legend in corrupt Greek characters, the two letters at the end opposite the chin being the same as those in the field of No. 6, which I read as *Shono* or *Shoho*, for *Shâhi*. The letters on the left at the beginning are the same as those on Figs. 18, 19, Plate IX., which I take to represent *Sio* for *Sri*. The intervening letters should give the name. *Rev.*—Fire altar, with two attendants facing it. Indian legend in two lines, one on each side, *Sri Yâdevi—mâna Sri*. The letters differ and are corrupt. Wilson, *Ariana Antiqua*, p. 402, reads doubtfully, *Srimad Deva Bhadra Sri*, and suggests that the last part may be *Khusru*. To the right and left are two short words in Pahlavi, which Thomas reads as *Punshamdât*, a faulty rendering of *Pûn shami dât*.
6	AR	46	Author, unique. Beardless head of king as on No. 5; legend also the same. *Rev.*—Fire altar and two attendants, the figure on the right being winged. Indian legend in two lines and short Pahlavi legends as on No. 5.

PLATE X.

Vasu Deva or Vakhu Deva.

No.	Metal.	Wt. Grs.	
7	AR	51	Author, 2 specimens; *Ariana Antiqua*, XVII. 8, p. 400. Beardless head of king, with large wings and crescents on head-dress, like the coins of Khusru II. Indian legend to right, *Sri Bahmana* (as read by Wilson), and to left *Vasu Deva*. The last two letters of *Bahmana* Wilson considers doubtful. I read tentatively *Vangâra* or *Chandâra*. *Vasu Deva* seems uncertain. Both Prinsep and Thomas read *Vakhu*; but as the Indian letters on these coins are very degraded, the letter might have been intended for a square ष *ṣ*, instead of स *s*. [See Thomas, *Pahlavi Coins of Early Muhummadan Arabs*.] There is a circular legend all round the piece, which no one has yet read. It appears to me to be very degraded Greek. I can see *Shono*. *Rev.*—Fire altar, with two attendants standing to front, with two short words in Pahlavi to right and left. Circular legend round the outside as on the obverse. The letter *B* occurs twice in this legend.
8	Æ	29	Author, unique. Beardless head of king, with winged head-dress surmounted by lion's head with mouth open; a javelin in left hand held upright before face. Symbol in field to left. *Rev.*—Fire altar and two attendants, with two Pahlavi words as on No. 7.

Khusru II. of Persia.

No.	Metal.	Wt. Grs.	
	AR		From Longpérier's *Médailles des Rois Perses*, Pl. XI., fig. 3, p. 78. Bearded head of the Sassanian king Khusru Parvez to the front, with a pair of wings on his crown. In the margin on each

PLATE X.

No.	Metal.	Wt. Grs.	
			of the four sides a crescent and a crown. Pahlavi legend to right, *Husrui Malkân Malkâ.* *Rev.*—Bust of the Indian Sun-god of Multân, with rayed head-dress. To the left, in Pahlavi, *haft-sih* = 37, the year of his reign = A.D. 627. N.B.—I ventured to suggest this identification of the rayed bust with the Sun-god of Multân eighteen years ago (*Archæol. Survey*, V., p. 123), because the same bust appears on the coins of *Shâhi Tigin* and *Vâsu Deva*, the actual kings of Multân.
			SHAHI TIGIN.
9	AR	52	Author, 26 specimens, an average weight 48 to 50 grains; see *Ariana Antiqua*, XXI. 22; E. Thomas, *Pahlavi Coins of Arabs*, p. 92. Beardless head of king, three-quarter face, with small moustaches; his tiara surmounted by a tiger's head and two trisuls; in field to right, three characters, which I take to be corrupt Greek for *Sri Shono*, the first being doubtful. Indian legend in circle outside which I have read tentatively, *Sri Hitivi-cha Airân-cha Parameswara Sri Shâhi TIGIN Devaja.* "The fortunate sovereign both of India and of Persia, the fortunate Shahi TIGIN, the Son of Heaven." *Rev.*—Male head to front, with rayed flames ascending to a point [the Sun-god of Multân = *Aditya*]. Pahlavi legend to left and right: To left—*Saf-Takhif-Tef* = *Sri Tigin-Devaja.* To right—*Takân Khorasân Malkâ* = *Tâki-Khorasân Malka.* N.B.—*Tâki* was the name of the Panjâb, of which *Tâki-shahr*, or *Taxila*, was the capital. It therefore represents *India*, the *Hitivi* of the Sanskrit legend, while *Khorasân* represents the *Airân*. By these readings, the Sanskrit and Pahlavi legends correspond

PLATE X.

No.	Metal.	Wt. Grs.	
			fairly well. I take this king to have been the founder of *Takinâbâd*, one of the two capitals of Zâbulistân. According to the Tabakât-i-Nasiri it was the "largest town in Garmsir." I infer that it was originally the *Hasalo* of the Chinese annals. It was taken from *Lak-lak* in the end of the ninth century, by the Safâri Yakub bin Lais. It then fell to the Ghaznavis, and in the twelfth century it belonged to the Ghoris, who pursued Bahram Ghaznavi to Takinâbâd.

VASU-DEVA.

No.	Metal.	Wt. Grs.	
10	Æ	52	Author, 4 specimens; see *Ariana Antiqua*, XVII. 9. Head of king, with a pair of large wings on head-dress, as on coins of Khusru Parvez. Two Pahlavi legends in inner and outer circles. Inner to left, × *Afzut.* Inner to right, *Saf Varsu Tef* = *Sri Vâsu Deva.* *Margin*—Saf Varsu Tef—Wahman × Multân Malkâ. "Sri Vâsu Deva, king of Bâhman and Multân." *Rev.*—Head of Sun-god as on No. 9. Indian legend to right—*Sri Vâsu Deva* (reversed). Pahlavi legend to left — *Tukân Zâülastân* (= India, Zabulistân). Margin—*Sapardalakhshân* = *Sapâdalaksha* (= Rajputâna). N.B.—I take *parda* to represent pâda, just as *Varsu* = Vâsu. On my other three coins, which I bought at the sale of the spare coins of the Masson Collection, there is a deeply stamped and well executed "boar's head." This may be seen in Wilson's plate, *Ariana Antiqua*, XVII. 9. He has made a mistake about the boar's head, as he describes the countermark as containing "illegible characters" (p. 400). Several of the Vasu Deva coins have the Indian legend written from right to left, as in

PLATE X. No.	Metal.	Wt. Grs.	
			my coin given in the plate. The coin in the British Museum has the name correctly written from left to right.
11	Æ	66	British Museum, unique. Beardless head of the king, three-quarter face, with a pair of small wings and two crescents on tiara, and large earring in ear; in the field to right, a small human figure lying on his back, with legs raised, and head also raised, and looking between his legs. To left, Pahlavi legend, unread. *Rev.*—Rayed head of Sun-god, as on Nos. 9 and 10. Pahlavi legends: Left—*Saparlakshan* = *Rajputana.* Right—*Zâülistan* = *Zabulistan.* Marginal legend not read.

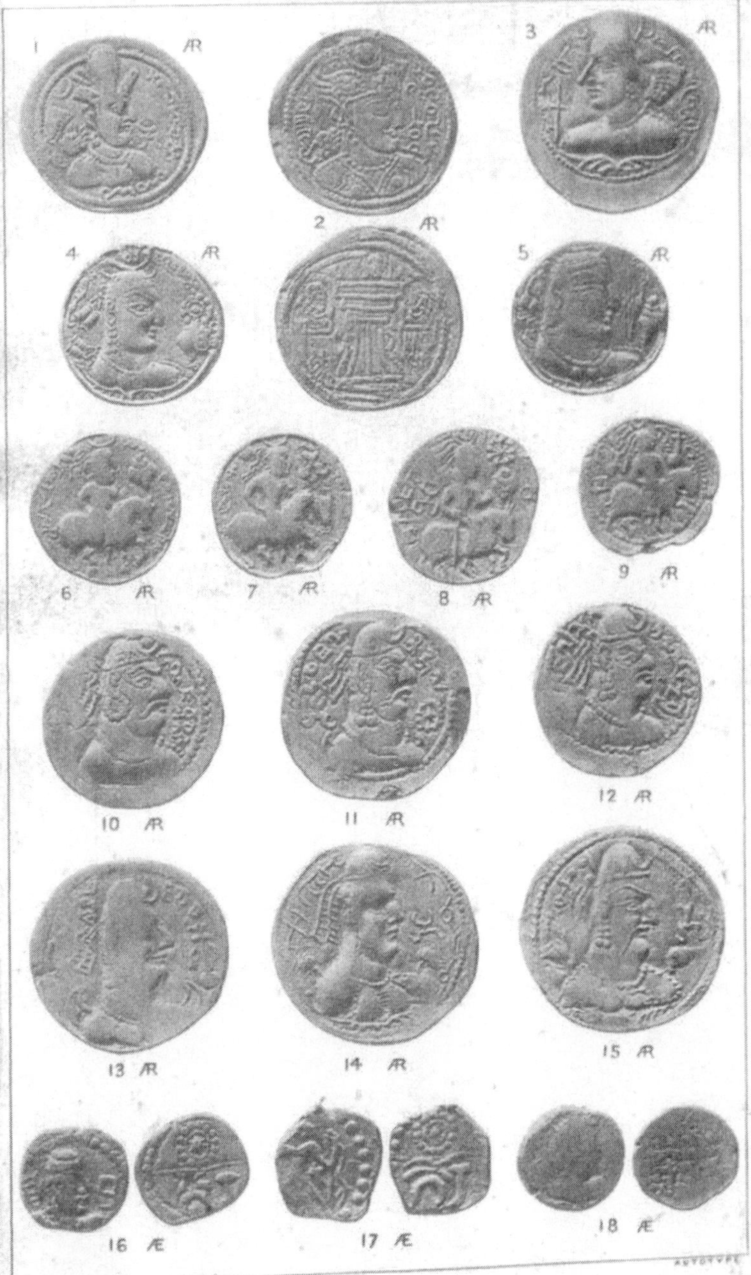

EPHTHALITES OR WHITE HUNS. — PLATE VII.

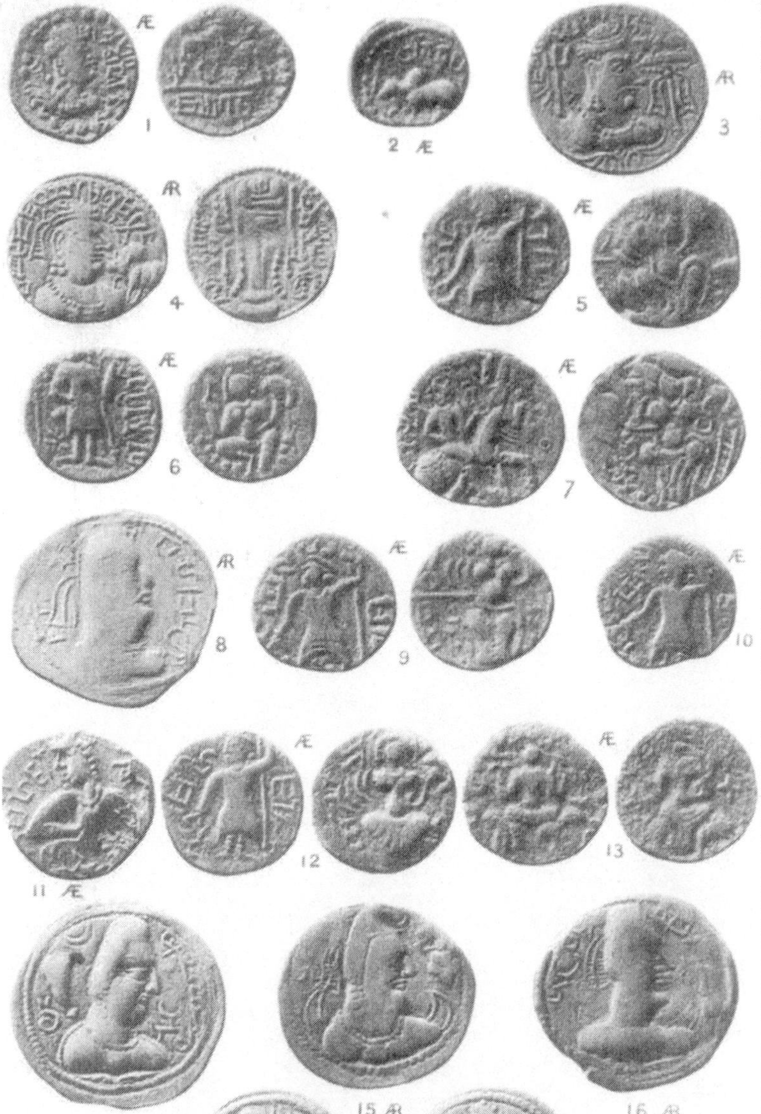

EPHTHALITES OR WHITE HUNS. PLATE VIII.

ERHTHALITES OR WHITE HUNS. PLATE IX.

EPHTHALITES OR WHITE HUNS. PLATE X.

INDEX.

Coin-legends are printed in *italics*.

M.

N.

P.

R.

S.